Teach Your Horse to Jump

W. J. W. FROUD

1972 EDITION

Published by

WILSHIRE BOOK COMPANY

12015 Sherman Road

No. Hollywood, California 91605

Telephone: (213) 875-1711

THOMAS NELSON AND SONS LIMITED

36 Park Street London W 1
PO Box 27 Lusaka
PO Box 18123 Nairobi
PO Box 21149 Dar es Salaam
77 Coffee Street San Fernando Trinidad

THOMAS NELSON (NIGERIA) LTD
PO Box 336 Apapa Lagos

THOMAS NELSON (AUSTRALIA) LTD
597 Little Collins Street Melbourne 3000

THOMAS NELSON AND SONS (SOUTH AFRICA)
(PROPRIETARY) LTD
51 Commissioner Street Johannesburg

THOMAS NELSON AND SONS (CANADA) LTD
81 Curlew Drive Don Mills Ontario

Printed by

HAL LEIGHTON PRINTING CO.
P. O. Box 1231
Beverly Hills, California 90213
Telephone: (213) 346-8500

This book first published 1971
© W. J. W. Froud 1971

ISBN 0 17 147206 3

CONTENTS

1 The First Stages   *page* 1

2 Loose Jumping   14

3 Early Mounted Training   19

4 Further Steps in Jumping   50

5 Show Jumping   65

6 Hunting   76

7 Point to Point Riding   81

8 Training for One- and Three-Day Events   86

9 Conclusion   98

   Index   101

Chapter 1

THE FIRST STAGES – LUNGEING
AND LOOSE JUMPING

To teach a horse anything the sensible trainer must have a knowledge of the animal's nature and of his characteristics. The horse is by nature a gentle creature, if unspoiled by man, but he is also timid, easily frightened and confused. It follows then that the trainer must be patient but firm, demanding little and explaining each step.

The horse has an excellent memory but very little reasoning power, so his training is based on an association of ideas. An elementary example of this principle is when we teach him to lead. We say 'Walk on!' and tap his flank with a whip. His natural instinct is to go away from discomfort or pain so he moves forward and instantly the trainer stops the whip action. The horse then learns to associate the voice with the whip and very soon there is no further need of the latter. This method applies throughout training, with, of course, many variations. The good trainer must be clever, watchful and imaginative, always ready to anticipate his horse and always prepared to 'give' to his horse the moment the horse 'gives' to him, whether working mounted or dismounted.

In this way a happy relationship will be established between horse and trainer. The trainer must gain the young horse's confidence; at the same time he must quietly insist

1

on obedience in all things, whether in the stable or during outside training. To get the best from him on the flat or over fences, a horse must be relaxed in mind and muscle. He cannot possibly be relaxed unless he is calm; he cannot be calm unless he is confident. Mind and muscle are inextricably bound together, and the horse will immediately stiffen under the influence of fear or apprehension. So the first task of the successful trainer is to engender confidence. Calmness and relaxation will follow.

We have said that the horse has a marvellous memory, unfortunately he remembers the bad things as well as the good. Acquired faults are the result of training, and if bad results are produced the trainer must look to himself and not to the horse for improvement. To teach good qualities requires tact and patience. One must go slowly, step by step, explaining in simple language what is required. If we are observant and watch the horse's ears and eye we can usually tell how far to go. A horse must never be punished if he fails to understand what is demanded; it is usually the rider's lack of skill in asking and not a direct disobedience.

It is the trainer that makes the horse. How often do we hear: 'Old so and so is a terrific trainer, he produces three or four good jumpers every year.' What I ask is: 'What happens to those three or four good horses in the second and third years?' Usually they are never seen again. No, the good and successful trainer is the one whose horses improve year by year and eventually reach the top. To quote a famous horseman of a previous generation: 'Stick to him till he does what you require, trusting nevertheless to time and not to violence.'

Now, let us say we are fortunate in having a young horse which we are going to school as a jumper. We know that all riding horses can be taught to jump even if only a comparative few reach the top class as show jumpers, but most horses, if they are schooled in a methodical and sensible manner, can reach a standard of jumping which will allow us to hunt in most countries with confidence and to enter various local competitions. This surely is what the vast majority require: a horse one can ride for pleasure. There is no great magic in schooling a horse up to this elementary standard. The principles involved are simple, and their correct application is well within the ability of the good average horseman. Let us therefore take our young horse through the various stages of training that will produce for us a pleasant ride and a consistent reliable jumper.

First, what is a young horse? If you are buying a horse it is best and most economic to look for a four-year-old. At this age a horse is ready to start serious training. At six or seven he will begin to reach his best; if he is well looked after he is in his prime from seven to fifteen years, and often much longer. But usually it is in the early years that the damage is done. No horse's bones are mature enough to start serious mounted training until he is four. If you buy at two or three a certain amount of training may be carried out, such as handling and quiet lungeing, but if you do anything more strenuous your horse is very liable to sustain permanent injury. Naturally, some breeders and dealers are only too ready to sell off two- and three-year-olds to save the expense of upkeep. But the fact is that before his fourth year a young horse is just not capable of standing up to hard work and his joints are still too soft to take the added weight of the rider during strenuous schooling periods, particularly over fences.

It is not part of my task in this book to discuss conformation, and it is said anyway that good jumpers come in all shapes and sizes, but one thing a trainer cannot do is alter a horse's nature. So a calm temperament and a bold outlook

3

are the first things to look for. The most reliable indication of disposition is the eye, which should be alert and friendly with no white showing.

From the moment of purchase every effort must be made to gain the horse's confidence. Hand feeding and quiet handling are essential. A quiet, calm stable produces calm and happy horses, and our training begins in the stable. Nevertheless, although we hand feed and handle our horse we do not pet him. A spoilt horse is as bad as a spoilt child, and from the beginning we must demand obedience in small things. He must learn to stand still to be haltered and rugged; he must learn to move over when told to do so. In fact, the more one talks to one's horse the better, but we must remember that his hearing is acute and that if we shout at him we will only make him frightened. One builds up a simple vocabulary by the intonation of the voice rather than by words, which in any case a horse cannot understand.

Before we start to work the horse his teeth and feet must be inspected. Many horses, through the ignorance of their owners, suffer from sharp teeth. How can a horse possibly be happy in his training if he is not happy in his mouth! A few minutes' work by a veterinary surgeon with a tooth rasp can make all the difference to a horse's comfort during training. Then his feet must be inspected by the blacksmith. If you intend to work him shod he must be shod up all round as soon as possible so that the feet may get over that slight initial soreness. You may decide to work him without shoes behind in the early stages, in which case the hind feet must be bevelled round with the rasp so that there is less risk of splitting and breaking.

A daily inspection by the trainer is a 'must'. Examine the legs, feet, back and mouth for signs of soreness or strain. The slightest sign of puffiness in a tendon, or of heat in the foot, must receive immediate attention. If neglected, irreparable harm may be done. Many unnecessary blemishes on young horses' legs are caused by ignoring these early signs of strain. Careful attention must also be paid to diet, particularly in these early stages. Too much corn or hard food, and a horse with the most equable temperament can be made nappy and unmanageable. The horse must be conditioned from the very beginning to be quiet and attentive.

The first step in training outside the stable is to teach the horse to lead well. Most horses that have been handled will follow quietly behind a human being, but we must now begin to ask more by getting the horse to walk boldly forward with the trainer walking beside his shoulder. By doing so we are beginning to impose our will and we are insisting on *forward* movement, which is the basis of all training. To carry out this task efficiently the horse must wear a well-fitting cavesson. The noseband must be well padded, and it must fit closely, so that it does not twist when the rein is applied to the centre 'D'. The throatlatch must fit low enough to stop the cheekpiece moving and so touching the horse's eye. A webbing lead rein or lunge rein with a light spring clip attachment should be clipped to the centre 'D'. For this work I prefer to use an ordinary schooling whip. It is easier to handle than a long whip, which is not necessary at this stage.

Now we are ready for our first lessons in obedience and forward movement. We start on the near side, which is usually the easiest side to lead from. The leading rein is lightly held in the left hand and the whip carried roughly parallel to the ground in the right, pointing to the rear. The lead rein is long enough for us to stand by the horse's shoulder without constraint on the nose. We ask the horse to 'Walk on!' in a brisk tone; this is accompanied by a gentle tap with the whip on the flank. The horse's natural instinct is to move away from discomfort, and in a surprisingly short time he will learn to move forward freely, also being helped by our urging him on with the voice reinforced by tactful taps with the whip.

The hand, which up to now has allowed the forward movement by being light and passive, now supplements the voice when we say 'Whoa!' or 'Halt!'. It is not necessary to jerk on the rein. While walking our contact with the horse is by the weight of the rein only. When we ask him to stop our hand resists the movement of the head and the horse eventually stops, but he must be given time and a few paces to do so. The horse's walk must be free and long striding and it follows, therefore, that the trainer must be in a fit condition to suit his walk to that of the horse; he must in no way impede its roomy stride.

This simple act of early obedience can be instilled into the young horse in a few lessons. Lessons should be short: fifteen to twenty minutes twice a day. When he will lead easily from the near side the same work should be done on the off side, changing over rein and whip. By gradually lengthening the rein and dropping farther behind the horse's shoulder we can soon have the horse working on a large circle with the trainer walking on a smaller circle. Eventually the trainer can stand still in the centre and a perfect circle can be obtained around him. All this work should be performed quietly and without fuss, and when we reach this point the horse will have learnt to associate the whip and hand with the voice. He will be afraid of neither, but he will respect both. This is the ideal basis on which to start more serious schooling.

At this stage an ordinary jointed snaffle may be fitted. It must be carefully adjusted, neither so high as to be uncomfortable, nor so low that the horse can get his tongue over the mouthpiece. Allow your horse to feed once a day in this snaffle; eating teaches him to keep his tongue below the bit.

LUNGEING – I do not intend to go into all the aspects of lungeing, but from the jumper's point of view many beneficial results can be achieved. Lungeing instils the habit of obedience. It improves the paces and develops muscles. It 'sows the seed of impulsion'. Furthermore, it allows us to introduce the horse to small fences without his having a weight on his back or suffering any interference from the rider. This maximum freedom over small fences is a very important start to jumping.

For lungeing we need a cavesson, as before, and a lunge rein of a good length, somewhere between 25 ft. and 30 ft. long. If you buy a lunge rein from a saddler without stipulating the length it will probably be a little under 20 ft., which is too short even for normal lungeing. For myself, I now carry a lungeing whip, although I do not expect to use it a great deal. Even so, it is necessary as a reminder, and it can be used to reinforce my orders if necessary. If and when it is used, the whip should be applied lightly and quickly below the hock with a minimum of noise and movement. It should never be cracked or swished. Practice is necessary, however, if one is to use a long whip efficiently. So one should spend some time flicking at a piece of paper on the ground before taking it near the pupil. For lungeing work the horse's forelegs should be protected with boots, as a young horse can easily become unbalanced and strike into himself, with disastrous results, when he is working on the circle.

Having taught the horse to walk quietly in front of you with a gradually lengthened rein, the walk on the circle follows quite naturally. And for the first few days he does nothing but this: walk and halt; walk and halt; stand still; then a pat and a quiet word from the trainer, and a change of rein to send him round in the opposite direction. I insist on my horse obeying these simple commands to walk, halt and stand: they are an essential part of his training. I have no patience with the person who allows himself to be dragged round on the end of a lunge rein while the horse 'lets off steam'. We all know that a young horse will often throw a buck through sheer exuberance, but to allow it to happen daily is to encourage bad habits. For young and inexperienced trainers who have no enclosed space in which to lunge, a ring of hurdles some 45 ft. in diameter in a quiet corner of a field gives much greater safety and a large measure of control. It may well be necessary to have an assistant to enforce one's commands; but with or without an assistant, the horse must be made to walk to order.

The walk should be at a calm and relaxed pace, but it must not be a lazy one. To walk well the horse must be allowed to lengthen his neck and to swing his head. This will produce an energetic, swinging stride without hurry. He must be allowed to carry himself, but with the rein control just strong enough to encourage his body to conform to the line of the circle. The same principles apply when we start to trot the horse: we want a calm but energetic pace with long roomy strides, with the horse learning to carry himself in balance on the line of the circle and on both reins. Lessons should continue to be of short duration; twenty minutes to half an hour twice a day is quite enough.

When the horse will walk, trot and halt happily to the word of command we may introduce a pole on the circle—preferably a painted one, solid and at least four inches in diameter because it must be heavy enough not to roll when knocked. This early introduction to the pole teaches the horse to respect a fence without being afraid of it. He will first learn

8

to walk over it and then to take it in his stride when trotting, without altering his stride. A second pole some $4\frac{1}{2}$ to 5 ft. away from the first can then be introduced, to be negotiated first at a walk and eventually at a trot. Above all, calmness and quietness must be maintained. To trot over two poles at this distance apart the horse must make a conscious effort

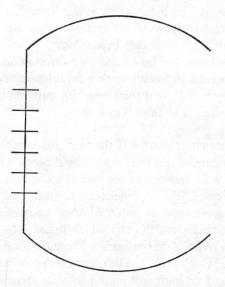

Fig. 1 The position of ground poles on a straight line for work on the lunge.

to balance himself in order to avoid knocking the poles. By encouraging him to do this we are teaching natural balance, impulsion, freedom of the shoulder and hock action. Introducing further poles should be done carefully. The poles must be placed in a straight line, and the trainer learn to move his horse on an ellipse so that he can trot his poles on the straight (Fig. 1). Trotting or jumping on the line of the circle calls for great suppleness and balance, and it would be asking too much of any horse at this stage.

If these simple lessons are carried out with patience, step by step, over a period of about six weeks we will have a horse that is calm, confident and obedient. The value of good lungeing for the young horse cannot be overestimated and the exercise can be reverted to at any time during his life. With excitable, nervous or badly-trained horses twenty minutes lungeing each day before riding is of tremendous value. Only harm can be caused by mounting an over-fresh, fretful or rebellious horse; work a troublesome horse on the lunge to begin with, and then give him quiet mounted work, still on the lunge, to calm him down.

JUMPING ON THE LUNGE – If the previous lessons have been thoroughly carried out the horse should now be going freely forward at walk and trot to the trainer's command. His walk should be calm, long and active; the trot should be brisk, showing a good rhythm, with the horse's body moving on the line of the circle, and he should walk and trot confidently down a line of poles on both reins. From here it is but a small step for the horse to take the last of the six poles, which should be raised to 2 ft. high and placed some 9 or 10 ft. from the fifth pole. The horse will trot into the line in his accustomed manner and hop over the last pole. It sounds a very simple operation, but the trainer does have a number of things to think about. First, if he uses a cavalletti as his last jump he must ensure that his lunge rein cannot catch in the cross-piece. Such a disaster could set the training back for a number of weeks. If the horse should lose confidence at this stage it would be a very serious matter, so the trainer must be doubly careful in his handling. When lungeing over fences the rein must be able to slide up and over smoothly, without any tension on the cavesson ring, and the horse's head and neck must be completely free throughout the jump. To ensure this a simple sliding wing can be made. If the stand is built to a height of 3 ft. it can be used for various types of fence, as shown in the diagram.

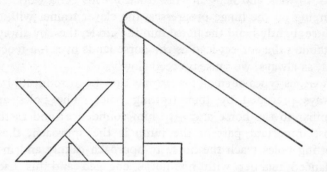

Fig. 2 Simple 3 ft. sliding wing used when jumping the horse on the lunge. There is no risk of the rein being caught on the upright.

As he lands over this first little jump the horse may well go into a canter stride, and nine times out of ten it will be a balanced canter stride with the correct leg leading. Up to now we have not cantered on the lunge, and for a number of good reasons. Attempting to canter too early on such a small circle places a tremendous strain on limbs that are not yet fit and hard. Also, ideally the horse should strike off from a balanced trot into a balanced canter on the correct lead with no increase of pace, and this is a difficult lesson to teach. What all too frequently happens is that the horse is driven faster and faster down onto his forehand with the trainer hanging on more and more tightly to the lunge line until the poor unbalanced horse eventually strikes off into a sprawling canter with the wrong leg leading. This does far more harm than good. Surely it gives the trainer much greater pleasure, and a greater sense of achievement, if he waits a little longer, allows the trotting poles to do their suppling and balancing work, and then lets the horse strike naturally into one or two strides of balanced canter, after which he can be brought back to walk and halt, and rewarded for his good work. As jumping on the lunge progresses, the clever trainer will, of course, lightly bend the horse into the circle, thereby always obtaining the correct lead as the horse lands over the fence. But, as always, we must proceed slowly.

Various types of small fences may now be introduced, but always preceded by four trotting poles. The poles are familiar to the horse and give him confidence; and as the most important part of the jump is the approach, these trotting poles teach the horse to approach calmly and in a balanced manner with his hocks engaged and his back relaxed. This is the best possible state for the horse to be in, and it enables him to learn how to round (or *bascule*) over his fences. When it is considered that this stage has been reached, the trotting poles may be removed, and small spread fences of up to 3 ft. in height and spread can be taken. All fences must be solid: a badly made fence, easily knocked down, teaches carelessness and disrespect. It is advisable to give jumping lessons at the end of the day, when the horse has had time tx settle to his work. It must be remembered also that increases in height and spread must be made gradually. When a young horse is jumping well the inexperienced but enthusiastic trainer is often tempted to raise or widen the fence just another three inches; but he should stop and wait for another day. It is natural to be impatient for progress, but to hurry any phase of training, most of all in jumping, is to push the young horse beyond his ability, running the risk of his losing confidence or becoming sore, which may well result in disobedience and refusals. Whatever the cause, if this happens the trainer has lost ground and his young horse has learned to shy at a fence. At the first sign of nervousness, loss of confidence, rushing or stopping, we must return to our trotting poles and the small familiar fences; otherwise we shall create problems that will undo all our patient preliminary work.

In these chapters I am concerned only with teaching the horse to jump, so we must assume that our horse has been backed and that elementary mounted training is proceeding during the lungeing-over-fences period.

Chapter 2

LOOSE JUMPING

When the horse goes well at walk and trot over poles on the ground, mounted work may be started. This should follow exactly the same lines as the lunge training: the same fences, the same poles used in the same place. The horse is a creature of habit, and seeing the same things in the same place will give him confidence. Mounted training over fences will be discussed in detail in later chapters.

Jumping on the lunge has great value, and many good lessons can be taught if these simple stages are gone through quietly and with patience. But lungeing over fences has its limitations, and the inexperienced trainer would be well advised to go very slowly, confirming each stage before progressing to the next. Use small spread fences, encouraging the horse to use himself, rather than attempting height, which might over-face him.

If the trainer has a number of horses that pass through his hands for schooling over fences, a loose manège is well worth building. Chasing horses down a straight lane of fences with shouts and cracking whips is a worthless exercise and does far more harm than good. Loose jumping must be planned and the horse must be trained to it, not frightened or bullied into it.

A properly built loose manège with curved ends and straight sides can be constructed inside any indoor riding school or, better still, erected permanently in an outdoor schooling area. A number of horses can then be handled daily with the minimum of fuss and with excellent results. The size of the manège is important. It must be constructed so that the whole operation can be controlled by one man – the trainer – but it must be long enough to take two upright fences on

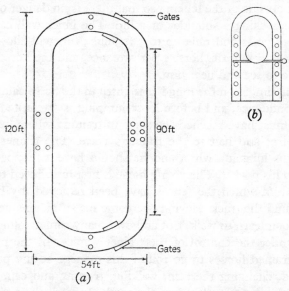

Fig. 3a Diagrammatic sketch of the ideal jumping lane.

Fig. 3b Sectional view of a pole and stand suitable for a jumping lane.

one side, 21 to 24 ft. apart, which is a distance that will give one canter stride between the two jumps for the average horse. (A refinement would be to make this distance adjustable, so that the number of strides between obstacles could be varied.) Also, a minimum of two straight cantering strides on either side of this double is needed. On the other side of

15

the manège an adjustable spread fence can be built. A small fence fixed at either end will deter the horse from rushing. All these fences need to be solid but portable (see diagram of jumping lane). Ideally, the outer wall of the manège should be about 6 ft. high, and it should act as a screen so that the horse is unable to see out. All construction posts should be on the outside of the fencing so that there is no danger of the horse knocking a shoulder or a hip. The inner wall can be made of posts and rails up to 5 ft. high; this will allow the trainer to watch the horse's performance, and the horse will be able to see and hear him.

Your aim, as on the lunge, is to instil in the horse calmness and confidence, and before loose jumping is attempted, the horse must have reached the stage in training where he will walk, trot and halt to the trainer's voice. The trainer will need his lungeing whip, and he should have a few oats or nuts in his pocket. The young horse is first introduced to the lane, from which the fences have been removed, by being led round the track. Having overcome his suspicions he will very soon learn to walk, trot and eventually canter round the lane under the control of the trainer's voice. In the past I have trained horses to go round this manège at any pace I wanted, changing the rein, walking, trotting and cantering over any obstacle placed in the track. Indeed, they can be made so calm and attentive that they will halt when approaching a fence if ordered to do so. But one must start right at the beginning again, going back to the poles on the ground. Then, when he is completely familiar with the manège and has begun to understand what is required of him, he will quickly learn to jump. As he did in the early days of lungeing, the trainer positions himself behind the horse's shoulder, with his whip held as for lungeing. He then moves on an inner line behind the horse, talking to him and quietly encouraging him to walk. The natural thing for the horse to do is to turn back to the gate through which he came, and this tendency must be checked with tact and quiet firmness. Any chasing with the whip or shouting is a bad start to a new lesson, and, in any case, excessive use of the whip will cause the young horse continually to look inwards and backwards in anticipation of its use, instead of looking forward to his fence. The object is to produce quiet unhurried jumping, so the procedure follows much the same steps as on the lunge until the trainer can stand in the middle of the manege with the horse listening to his every word and jumping free at trot or canter over parallel rails and doubles. It cannot be stressed too much that fences must be raised gradually and that spreads are more important than trying to get high jumps. A horse will use himself much more over a spread fence of, say, 2 ft. 6 in. high and 3 ft. wide than he will over a straight-up-and-down fence that is much higher, and the former will do far more towards encouraging the desirable rounded style.

Too much jumping at any one time only serves to make the horse careless and unenthusiastic, so after a few rounds of the manège the trainer should quietly halt him and reward him with a lump of sugar or a few oats before going round on the other rein. The bigger the fences the shorter the period of jumping should be if the horse is not to be made sour and resentful. If it is used in this way the jumping lane will day by day improve the horse's confidence, style and scope.

Once this phase is established, all types of fence may be introduced into the loose manege, but they should all be slightly smaller than the plain rails used previously. Small gaily-coloured walls, bales of straw, twine with paper tied to it and dangling down, a variety of poles and a piece of blue canvas to represent a stretch of water – these are all fences of a kind that can easily be contrived, and they are a good preparation for the various obstacles that the horse is certain to encounter later on when he has to jump in the show ring.

There are trainers who say that loose jumping is a waste of time, but I believe that if every horse were to start his jumping training loose there would be far more free-going horses in the hunting field, and in the riding world as a whole. Riding over fences is a partnership, and the best of riders make mistakes, especially riding across country. It is then that the horse with scope, developed and encouraged when jumping free, will take over and get the rider out of trouble – provided that the latter can learn to leave his horse alone at the moment of crisis. When jumping free the horse learns to balance himself, he develops his muscles, and he learns to adjust his stride and to use his head and neck without fear of interference from the rider. Some of the more expert show jumping riders aim at complete domination of pace and stride control, particularly at puissance standard, but when a mistake is made disaster follows. This more advanced standard will be discussed in later chapters, however. In my experience, loose jumping is an excellent foundation for the production of consistent performers in any field and it is a pity that more horses do not receive a thorough and systematic jumping education in which this system of schooling plays so important a part.

Chapter 3

EARLY MOUNTED TRAINING

The young jumper's basic training on the flat will proceed along conventional lines, and for at least the first six months he will have his lunge lessons before being ridden. This instils the habit of obedience, it helps him to relax, and it prepares his mind and his body for the elementary mounted work that is to follow. Ideally, the young horse's day should be divided up so that he never does anything for too long. Monotony will lead to lack of interest or rebellion, both of which are undesirable, whereas variety produces an active mind and therefore a better physical performance. The horse that is worked for one hour in the morning and then looks at a blank wall for the next twenty-three will not be a happy horse and the usual result of keeping horses idle for too long each day is the development of stable vices such as weaving, wind-sucking, crib-biting and kicking.

All work and training will depend entirely on the condition and temperament of each individual horse, and care over what he eats and how he eats it is vital in the early training stage. The job of the trainer is not only to produce a well-schooled horse, but also to build up a sound, healthy constitution and a calm disposition; indeed, if he fails in the second task he will certainly fall short in the first. The outline programme of training for each day might then be as follows:

9.00 a.m. 20 minutes work on the lunge
10.00 a.m. half an hour of quiet hacking
10.40 a.m. 20 minutes schooling in manège
2.00 p.m. 20 minutes lungeing, mainly work over poles

All mounted work in the early stages must be at a walk, except for the occasional slow trot. The half-hour hack should be in the company of a trained horse ridden by an assistant, and it is a very valuable part of the training. It is excellent for the young horse's health; and by following the older horse over varying types of country, broken ground, etc., he will gain confidence. I would recommend that this programme, in outline, should be adhered to throughout the first six months of training. Obedience to the simple aids will gradually be gained by performing straightforward figures and exercises, and, as they are confirmed in the horse, the degree of difficulty involved in the work on the flat and over fences can be increased; but for the first three months at least there should be no mounted jumping or cantering.

Before discussing in detail the work on the flat it might be as well to consider the qualities and ability of the good trainer. Far too many horses are spoiled through lack of thought and understanding on the part of the trainer. A good schoolteacher is one who understands and is in sympathy with a child's mentality. So it must be with the trainer of the horse – even more so, because in the beginning he does not understand our language. It takes time to build up the system of signals that will produce the right reflex actions in the horse. So first and foremost a trainer must have an understanding of the horse's thought processes and his instincts. We have mentioned the horse's wonderful memory, on which we rely tremendously in our training, but we must not credit the horse with reasoning power. He is unable to connect cause and effect unless they occur simultaneously. If a horse is to be punished, he must be punished *immediately* after the offence; to defer the punishment for even so short a time as half a minute is sheer stupidity on the part of his trainer, because the horse will then be quite incapable of understanding the reason for the punishment!

Patience and tact are very necessary attributes of the good trainer, and if he is to gain the horse's confidence he must be good humoured, calm and confident himself. He must be reasonable in his demands and be satisfied with a little progress each day. In short he must be a 'thinking' rider, alert and attentive, always watching his horse's expression during schooling; his seat, with his legs close to his horse's sides, should always be ready to anticipate a movement. If he hacks out in a sloppy manner his horse will become sloppy. This will lead to disobedience and to the development of a nappy animal. Unless the trainer has learnt self-discipline he cannot hope to discipline his horse. Finally, the trainer must be physically fit and a reasonably good horseman, with a supple and well-balanced seat that is absolutely independent of the reins.

THE SEAT – Having mentioned the importance of the seat let us consider it a little further. The majority of riders never get beyond the elementary stage. They learn enough to be competent and to enjoy themselves, but no more, and unfortunately many elementary riders attempt to school horses without thought of their own ability. The results are seldom happy. Few riders can truly say that their seat in the saddle is completely independent of the reins and that their body is always in balance whatever the horse may be doing. This condition of being in balance with the horse at all times is the key note of good riding. It means learning to sit in the right place, and to develop balance, suppleness and the right body muscles so that one can stay there whatever happens. The right place, of course, is as near to the withers as possible. This is where the horse is best able to carry weight and where the rib cage is strongest; farther back, towards the loin, the structure of the back is weaker. In addition this position near the withers is the only place on the horse's back where the rider feels the least disturbance from the animal's movement and where the horse is least affected by any untoward movement of the rider. It is only when the rider has developed a really deep seat that he can truly be 'at one' with his horse.

To acquire this deep seat the rider must be supple – in the back, hips, knees and ankles. But it is a controlled suppleness. Only by having a straight back can one be truly supple. The first obstacle to the achievement of this suppleness is the habit of gripping with the knees. This must stiffen the knee joint and cause the rider to squeeze up out of the saddle, when exactly the opposite effect is required. Gripping is a momentary affair, and when it is used it should start with the inside of the calf and become, eventually, a subconscious reflex action. The next aid to true suppleness is correct balance. At the halt and at the slower paces one should sit on the seat bones, placed well forward in the lowest part of the saddle, the thigh and knee at a natural comfortable angle to give support and lying as close to the saddle as possible, but *without gripping*. This closeness and adherence becomes greater as the rider's muscles develop, but any attempt to force the process will cause stiffness. With a supple knee and ankle the lower leg will go into the right place and stay there, close to the horse's side, with the rider's heel under the animal's shoulder. With the seat correctly positioned the stirrup leather will hang vertically and the rider will then be in true balance. If the lower leg goes forward he will be behind the movement; if the lower leg goes back, with the heel up, he will be in front of the movement; in either case he will be out of balance.

With the rider sitting in the manner described he is able to use his stirrups correctly; after all, they are there for his comfort and to make his position more secure. By having the stirrup iron on the ball of the foot, and by developing a supple knee and ankle joint, a varying proportion of the rider's weight will sink into the stirrup iron. If the knee and ankle are stiffened, we merely push the body away from the saddle.

The length of the stirrup will vary according to the activity at the time. When schooling on the flat, where maximum use of the seat and the lower leg is necessary, a longer leather is desirable, whereas moving across country at greater speeds, with sudden changes of pace and direction, and perhaps jumping, calls for a shorter leather, which gives greater mechanical advantage and enables the rider to stay in balance. The two extremes are the dressage rider at one end of the scale and the flat race jockey at the other, but the principles of the supple, balanced seat remain the same. Without it there is a lack of unity with the horse, and the would-be trainer will never achieve the hoped-for results.

THE HANDS – The first requisite of good hands is the achievement of a supple, balanced and independent seat. The second is softness – soft elbows, supple wrists and fingers. If the hands are to convey meaning to the horse then they must avoid all involuntary movement. We so often hear the cry: 'Keep your hands still!'; it should be: 'Keep your rein still!' The hands should be sensitive to the horse's mouth, and they are only 'still' relative to the mouth. Only by maintaining light and elastic contact can our wishes be conveyed clearly and accurately.

THE LEGS – Almost as much damage can be done by the involuntary movement of the lower leg as by the unsteady hand. The rider whose heel is continually tap, tap, tapping at every stride succeeds only in deadening the very sensitive skin just behind the girth. The primary function of the legs is to create and maintain impulsion, and to do this the inside of the calf and heel should lie close to the horse's side. When used it travels less than half an inch and is used quickly and lightly. If the young horse does not respond then the action is reinforced with a touch of the schooling whip. The more advanced the horse and its rider become the lighter the contact with the leg, and the more active will the horse be in response. Throughout this operation the heel is kept just below the toe, so that the ankle does not lose its elasticity, but it is necessary for the calf muscles to be braced.

SCHOOLING ON THE FLAT – In recent years more and more riders, both amateur and professional, have begun to realise that a certain amount of systematic schooling will improve the performance of the riding horse. Unfortunately, the word 'dressage' was used to describe this work, and the majority of people shied away from it as something connected with high school riding. Nothing could be further from the truth. The first year of schooling, starting with work in hand and on the lunge and then on the horse's back, is aimed at producing a horse that is calm and confident, whose balance has been adjusted so that he can carry the rider, whose muscles are developed so that he moves with a natural carriage without leaning on the bit, goes freely forward and has learnt to obey the elementary aids.

In this first year we must watch carefully his physical and mental development. He should be gay but obedient, both in the stable and outside. He should work quietly to both reins on the lunge and he should jump small fences both on the lunge and in the loose manège. He should stand still when being mounted and dismounted. In his work outside he should walk and trot quietly away from and towards home, down country lanes, across fields, up and down gentle slopes. He should stand when a gate has to be opened, and he should canter on selected ground without excitement, both in company and alone. He should go boldly over rough ground and jump small natural obstacles. In his school work his basic paces of walk, trot and canter should be even, energetic but calm. He should carry out simple school movements in a balanced and supple manner. He will be capable of jumping a variety of small coloured fences, placed at different distances, both from trot and canter. Where most would-be trainers fail is in demanding more than the young horse is physically capable of giving. Building and developing the right muscles involves slow and patient work.

This then is our aim for the first year. Let us see how we achieve it.

In the early mounted work the link between the trainer on the ground and on the horse's back is the voice. So the voice is used a great deal to begin with – to obtain elementary obedience to hand and leg, to calm and encourage. We have mentioned earlier that the horse's hearing is acute, so there is no need for loud noises of any kind, they only tend to upset and confuse. In fact, a great deal of our efforts must go towards keeping the young horse calm in the first few months of his training. Horses that become excited from fear are unreliable, particularly in their consistency over fences; they will also use up too much energy, and in a test of stamina, such as a three-day event, they will soon tire.

A good example of this fear is shying. It is quite useless getting angry and beating a horse for shying, and this is usually the reaction with the majority of riders. It only causes the horse to associate pain with the object. If it is persisted in, the final result will probably be a nappy horse. Shying can be overcome only by the rider sitting calmly but firmly, with his hand on the horse's neck and using his voice quietly to urge the horse forward. Most nervous habits – shying, prancing, fidgeting – are caused by lack of work. Long, steady, regular exercise is the cure for many troubles, both inside and outside the stable.

THE WALK – A great deal of early work is done at the walk, and the aim should be to develop a long low striding pace, calm but active. The walk is a pace of four-time and should have a regular, even beat. Now, at a walk a horse swings his head, which also oscillates slightly from side to side. The rider should do nothing to impede this natural movement, so most of the walking should be done on a long rein, with the rider preserving the 'soft' elbow and following the movement with his hands. In this way the horse will be encouraged to activate the hindquarters without restriction.

When a change of pace is required a shorter rein is necessary, and there should be a quiet closing of the rider's legs followed by a little more acceptance of the bit on the part of the horse. Having got this acceptance, a resisting hand will produce a halt, or a light quick leg aid will take the horse into trot. This work at the walk is very important – calmness is vital – but the trainer must never lose sight of the fact that free forward movement is the aim. So the horse must be encouraged to go resolutely forward, in front of the legs, and forward into contact with his bit, the leg being supported by the schooling whip when necessary. Any change of direction is done with an open rein with little or no backward tension.

Fairly early in this phase a few poles, coloured and plain, should be laid on the ground in convenient parts of the schooling area. At the end of the lesson, when the horse is calm, he should be allowed to walk over them; but remember that the poles must be heavy and not easily moved. This work has already been done on the lunge, so there should be no difficulty, and very soon the horse will walk over the rails without any change of pace, but with a slight lowering of the neck, which is desirable. Next put the poles into a grid, 5 ft. apart, as on the lunge, and soon he will be walking down six poles quite calmly. This is a good exercise in helping him to adjust his balance and develop muscle.

It is also at the walk that we begin lessons in lateral suppleness. To change direction smoothly, quickly and without loss of impulsion the horse must be truly supple to the right and left, and this work starts at the walk. The trainer must always insist that his horse goes smoothly through any turn or circle, with his hind feet following in the track of his forefeet, and looking in the direction he is going. We also achieve the beginning of longitudinal suppleness at the walk by asking the horse to lengthen and shorten his stride. This is best done when working in the open, up and down hills, etc.

The walk, rather than a faster pace, is used to explain new exercises to the horse in a calm and unhurried manner. Later on we will jump from the walk to make him use his hocks and to discourage rushing. The walk is a most valuable pace if used wisely.

THE TROT – The trot has been called by many experts the schooling pace, and there is no doubt that a great deal of useful work can be done at this pace. There are a number of reasons for this. The trot is a naturally even pace of two-time, and with a little development it becomes regular, the horse moving with natural balance and impulsion. It is from the trot that the sensible trainer does most of his early jumping. Some professional trainers ignore this pace and attempt to develop a short school canter straight away, frequently with disastrous results. The horse loses elasticity, scope and natural head carriage if the trot and jumping from the trot are not fully used. Another point of great importance is that at the trot the horse's head remains comparatively still, whereas in walk and canter it oscillates. This steadiness of the head makes it easier for the rider to maintain the light, unvarying contact with the mouth that is so vital at this stage of training. Indeed, it is such an easy pace to ride that the sensible rider need do very little beyond allowing the pace to develop by just concentrating on obtaining a slow but active rhythm, aiming at a perfect two-time pace of about seven miles an hour.

Until the horse is strong enough and sufficiently supple the rising trot should always be employed, the diagonals being changed at regular intervals so that the horse is encouraged to move evenly without any tendency to be one-sided. This rhythmic pace should become second nature to trainer and horse, whether working in the school or in the open country, and only when the horse begins to swing his back and develop his natural carriage should the sitting trot be attempted.

The young horse's head carriage must be carefully watched, particularly at this stage. He should be allowed to carry his head naturally, which in the vast majority of cases means that it will be held fairly low with the neck extended. The trainer should maintain a light elastic contact with the the mouth at all times, except when allowing the horse to rest. The young horse soon learns to rely on this contact, and this is the beginning of acceptance of the bit. As he develops muscle, strength and energy so will his hocks begin to come further under him, and his head and neck will gradually be carried higher, but nothing must be done to hurry this natural process.

Work over poles on the ground will be carried on at the ordinary trot, as at the walk, and soon the young horse should be trotting down six poles on the ground calmly and without fuss. The rhythm must be the same but the action must be robust, with the head lowered and the neck extended, and with the whole outline of the horse giving the impression of rounding the back from head to tail. The trotting poles should not be higher than six inches or farther apart than 5–6 ft., depending on the horse's stride. The rider's role is to maintain the rhythm of the pace, allowing the horse to extend his head and neck, and to stay in rising trot in the early stages. Work at the trot must also aim at lateral and longitudinal suppleness, increased obedience to hand and leg, and, most-important it must aim at free forward movement.

To move really fast through a sharp corner as in a speed competition a horse must be very supple, and to achieve equal suppleness to the right and left a great deal of work on the circle must be done. This can be quite difficult for the horse. To do it well he must bend the whole of his body to conform to the line of movement. His spine, between withers and loins, is fairly rigid, having little lateral flexibility, but much can be done to supple the neck and loin muscles. When circling to the right the muscles of loin and neck on that side contract and the muscles on the outside extend. By working to both sides we improve the strength and suppleness of these muscles. Also, on the circle the inside hind leg must come more under the body to take a greater share of weight and to deliver more impulsion. Working on circles, the action of both hind legs is stimulated and made stronger. The smaller the circle the more difficult the exercise will be; to make it easy for the horse, we start work on a large circle, at least twenty metres in diameter. We insist on an active trot, and by careful application of hand and leg the horse is encouraged to look slightly in towards the circle so that his body conforms to the line of movement. Most horses are stiffer on one side than the other. The trainer will soon discover his horse's stiff side, and again, to make the exercise easy for the horse, he will work him on his best side first; only when he is warmed up and going well will he attempt to work on the difficult side.

Riding on these circles should be continued until the horse is really swinging his back and flexing his neck muscles to the left and right without stiffness. The head carriage will still be fairly low, but the trainer should soon be able to do sitting or rising trot, at will, without altering the head carriage or the rhythm of the pace. When this can be done a milestone has been reached in the training and it is a great indication of improved suppleness and strength.

Work on the circle must, however, be alternated with work on straight lines, and here again we can meet with difficulty – it is so much easier to achieve lateral suppleness than longitudinal suppleness. First the horse must be taught to adjust his balance by work over undulating country, and in the manège by increase and decrease of pace. In these exercises we insist on immediate response to the leg aids but only ask for a gradual response to the hand aids. The trainer must remember that the horse's head and neck are used as a balancing pole and that any sudden restriction or pull by the hand will set up a resistance in the mouth. All decreases of pace must therefore be gradual, giving the horse time to use his hocks and to adjust his balance. But frequent changes of pace, termed transitions, must be practised: from halt to walk; walk to halt; walk to trot; trot to walk to halt; halt to trot – all achieved without swinging the hindquarters and with a still head carriage, the trainer's hand light and his legs and body doing most of the work. Within a few months, response to the leg will be immediate, and contact with the horse's mouth will be light and confident.

To improve fluid balance and obedience to hand and leg, lengthening and shortening the stride at the trot should now be practised. We begin by asking the horse to lengthen his stride. His natural reaction is to quicken the pace, but this we do not want. We want to achieve a lengthened stride with a slower rhythm, and this calls for a harmonious application of hand and leg. In rising trot the trainer must use his legs softly in rhythm with the stride; this will encourage extra hock action. At the same time he will open his fingers and allow the horse to extend his neck for two or three strides only; the legs will then cease their action and the fingers can close again. This exercise, carried out with tact and patience, will not only produce a lengthened stride but will also take the horse more onto the bit, and after a surprisingly short time he will begin to flex a little. We have already begun to obtain a certain amount of lateral flexion on our circles, and now, in this exercise, begins the direct flexion. But be careful not to ask too much. If any attempt is made to shorten the stride at this stage there will be evasions and resistance from the mouth and hindquarters. The danger signal is always given by the horse; resistance in the mouth, and/or unsteady head carriage, shows the wise trainer immediately that he has tried to go too far.

Work on circular tracks and on straight lines can now be combined. A few strides of extended trot followed by a circle in ordinary trot, first to the right, then to the left, will develop hock action, improve balance and suppleness and strengthen neck, back and loin muscles; all very necessary to produce balance and speed of movement. These exercises should gradually be utilised on circles, inclines, serpentines, etc.

The trainer must nevertheless work accurately and must always ride to markers. Even when not working in a manège one should fix the eye on a distant object when riding in a straight line, or pick out markers in a bush or a fence when riding on a circle. Accurate riding is essential to obedience.

Short but frequent rest periods must be given during all phases of training. The young horse's neck muscles, particularly, tire very quickly, and he must be allowed to extend the neck and walk on a long rein as an exercise. When standing still, complete freedom of the head and neck should be given. Each period of concentrated schooling should be of short duration. Most of our training at this time is spent in long walks and very slow trots, across country where possible, designed to strengthen and harden the horse's muscles. No work in canter can be attempted until a fair measure of fitness has been attained. An unfit horse is far more prone to injury than a fit one.

LATERAL MOVEMENT – Some experienced trainers say it is quite unnecessary for a jumper to be taught to move laterally away from the leg, but in my view any exercise that will increase the activity of the hindquarters and improve the trainer's control of them must be of value.

It is at this early stage that we teach the first simple movement of turning on the forehand. This is purely an exercise to teach the horse to move his quarters laterally away from the leg. The first lesson is given dismounted. With the horse standing even, hold the cheek-piece in the left hand and just touch the horse behind the girth with the schooling whip: he will move laterally away, crossing the near hind in front of the off. With a little patience and a reward at each step our horse will soon perform a quarter turn. To carry out the exercise when mounted, walk forward a few steps and halt, ask the horse too look to the left, apply the left leg with intermittent pressure until the horse moves his quarters. He then steps round a quarter circle, with the rider's right leg controlling the movement. As soon as he has done so, move forward immediately. The activity of the hindquarters must always be maintained, or half the value of the exercise is lost. Although the inside foreleg is the pivot of this movement it should not remain rooted to the ground; ideally it moves in the rhythm of the walk. On no account must the horse be allowed to step backwards during this movement.

THE CANTER – Most trainers and riders attempt to canter their horses too soon, and this is why so much disobedience and over-excitement takes place at this pace. The first point for the trainer to remember is that the change in rhythm from two- to three-time causes a drastic change in the head movement. At the trot the horse's head is still, but as he strikes off into a canter it begins to swing, and the action is very accentuated in the young horse. This natural swing must be allowed or evasions will be set up in the mouth and quarters. The early canter will be a long low stride with an extended neck postion, and again we must not alter this posture until the horse strengthens up and we are able to engage his hindquarters and obtain a more balanced pace. To canter true the horse must canter with the inside foreleg leading followed by the inside hind. This enables him to turn in a balanced manner and to move fast through corners, an absolute essential in a good jumper. Some trainers state that when first cantering it does not matter which leg the horse leads on. To my way of thinking this is asking for trouble. Why teach bad habits that must be corrected later? If care is taken to position the horse properly there should be little difficulty in obtaining the correct lead. When a horse canters on the circle left his near fore is naturally in front of his off-side one, and, just as naturally, he will carry his quarters slightly to the left. If, therefore, the horse is placed in this position *before* the aid is applied there should be no difficulty in obtaining a correct strike-off. So place your horse on the corner correctly bent in this way before giving the canter aid. The aid is the simple diagonal one that is used throughout the training. It is the emphasis in application that is important. As always, the inside hand asks him to look to the left; the outside hand allows the movement and controls the pace; the inside leg then acts strongly on the girth to maintain impulsion while the outside leg, placed behind the girth, signals the canter by giving a little nudge.

The canter is best achieved in the early stages from a balanced trot rather than from a walk, but difficulty is often experienced, particularly with children's ponies, when the horse runs on in an unbalanced manner, going more and more on the forehand. This occurs when the horse has not been sufficiently schooled to obey hand and leg and is really just not ready to canter. If, however, the inexperienced trainer has difficulty, the pace can be achieved quite easily and in a balanced manner by the use of cavalletti as explained previously.

The cavalletti work should now have reached the stage

where the horse can trot calmly but actively down six poles, spaced about 5 ft. apart, in rising trot. If a cavalletto, raised to about 2 ft., is placed between 9 and 10 ft. away from the trotting grid, as when the horse was working on the lunge, he will hop over it without trouble, although the rider must, of course, take care to allow the horse complete freedom of head and neck, and he must bend his body slightly forward to stay in balance. This is a simple enough exercise, but it represents the first mounted jump, and if the preliminaries

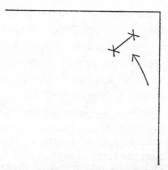

Fig. 4 Cavalletto placed on the corner to encourage the canter lead on the correct inside leg.

have been carried out thoroughly it can be accomplished without fuss.

Now, if this raised cavalletto is placed across a corner (Fig. 4) and is approached at a slow trot, the aid to canter being given as the horse takes off, a balanced strike-off with the correct leg leading is invariably achieved. Very soon, of course, we can dispense with the pole.

Cantering should be practised on large circles with frequent transitions to trot. If there is any sign of fuss or excitement during these canter exercises the trainer must return to the walk to calm his horse before trying again. The better bred the horse and the more courageous he is, the more careful the trainer must be. Gradual introduction of canter work over cavalletti has, in itself, a calming effect and, of course, it improves suppleness, increases confidence and prepares the horse for bigger fences.

The procedure is as follows: always use at least four poles for your trot approach to the first fence. The approach to a fence is the most important part of the jump, and these trotting poles continue to encourage the horse to come in

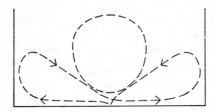

Fig. 5 School figures performed at trot. A valuable exercise is to shorten the stride on the track along the wall and extend it on the diagonal tracks. The circle, which can be ridden off the diagonal, is executed in a shortened trot.

calmly and in a balanced manner, with the hocks engaged and the back relaxed: this is the best possible state for him to be in, and it will encourage him to bascule over his fence. The rider should shorten his stirrup leathers one or two holes at this stage to give himself a greater mechanical advantage over the small fences he is about to tackle without materially altering his seat. The first small jump should be about 9 to 10 ft. away from the last trot pole and about 2 ft. high. The rider must now sit in balance with the minimum movement, letting the poles do all the work. The two things best calculated to put a horse off jumping at this stage are

(1) the weight of the rider banging down on his loins, or (2) a heave in the mouth at the critical moment by an unyielding hand.

Stillness in the rider is therefore essential. He must remain in balance over the trotting poles, placing his shoulders a little more forward, and putting a little more weight on his knee and thigh and down onto the stirrup irons. As his horse takes off the angle between the body and thigh closes, and the hand, with opening fingers, follows the movement of the head and neck. The legs remain close to the horse's side, with the stirrup leathers vertical, and the seat close to the saddle. Over the poles and the small jumps the rider's role is a passive one. His important tasks are connected with his actions before and after the fence. In the first place he must continue to ride his horse correctly through the corners and maintain a good rhythm in the approach, and after negotiating the fence he must ensure that his horse continues straight for at least three lengths before making a correct turn to right or left. Slipshod methods will inevitably lead to bad habits creeping in, so one must continue to ride accurately on the flat and above all to ride forward.

Now, the fence can be made into a parallel, 2 ft. high and 2 ft. apart. This calls for more effort from the young horse, and he will be obliged to round his back and extend his neck to a greater extent. He may canter a few strides after the jump and should be allowed to do so, the rider returning to a trot on a straight line and making sure that the canter strides are well balanced. A second parallel pair of rails can now be placed 18 to 21 ft. away from the first, the object being to obtain one canter stride between fences. This will entail the use of the rider's legs between fences in rhythm with the stride. There should be no sudden thump in the ribs on take-off; all that is needed are two squeezes, one for the stride and one for the take-off. When these two fences can be negotiated calmly with a confident canter stride in between, add a third pair of rails, this time with a little more distance between them. How great a distance depends very much on the stride of the individual horse: 18 ft. is short, 21 ft. is average and 24 ft. is quite long when the approach is still made from trot. But whatever distance is decided upon, it should be varied so that the horse learns to adjust himself to the problem presented, sometimes lengthening and some- times shortening his stride. There are many combinations that may be used: 33 to 35 ft. will give two, 45 ft. three non- jumping strides. However you adjust your rails, make certain your horse takes off cleanly from his stride, without putting in a short one, and that he maintains his rounded back. This is vital: if you ask too much he will flatten his back, become excited and unsteady. Any sign of excitement is an indication that the trainer is going too fast and that he should return to the previous stage.

FURTHER WORK ON THE CIRCLE – Work at the canter should continue on large circles. Riding in circles always has a calming effect, and we are much more likely to get continued obedience in the strike-off.

To improve suppleness and to increase the activity of the hindquarters, smaller circles may now be practised at the trot. A more balanced pace is required for these, and the horse has to be taught to shorten his base by bringing his hocks still further under his body. This action will produce greater energy with a lighter forehand and a correspondingly raised head carriage. It is best achieved by the trainer riding in sitting trot, when he will be closer to his horse and able to exert greater influence through his seat. Nevertheless the seat must still be very light, just sending the horse forward into a lightly resisting hand. In this way an energetic rhythm is produced that will be near to true collection. These smaller circles must, however, be approached gradually, or there will be a loss of impulsion and resistance from mouth or quarters. In training the horse no exercise is of benefit unless the rhythm is maintained to encourage the forward urge.

These exercises can be started by riding half circles, using the corner to help the correctness of the figure. (Fig. 5). The

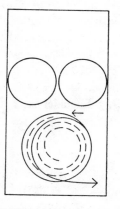

Fig. 6 The figure 8 and the spiral. In the latter the aim is to enter the movement at balanced trot and to leave in extension.

half circles and circles can be made large at first and smaller as the horse's suppleness and balance improves, but throughout the exercises great attention must be paid to the correct bend of the horse. At this stage the whole body will begin to bend round the rider's inside leg; it is the leg that works and produces the bend, the hand asking for the flexion to right and left as the direction changes.

Another exercise that assumes greater importance in later training is the figure eight in balanced trot, done as shown in Fig. 6. As always, the body must follow the line of movement, and care must be taken to ensure the correct change of bend on the centre line.

The 'spiral' is an excellent exercise, provided that the rider does not close the circle too abruptly and is able to maintain the same rhythm and impulsion. The horse should be taken into this movement in balanced trot and come out of it aiming at an extended trot. This gradual suppling of the body to the right and left by work on circles of various sizes leads us inevitably to the best of all suppling movements and that is the shoulder-in.

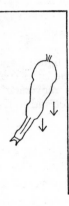

Fig. 7 Shoulder-in.

The shoulder-in is a movement on two tracks, the horse's body being flexed throughout its length away from the movement, progressing sideways by crossing the inside hind leg and inside foreleg in front of its outside legs. The hind feet remain in the track and the forefeet are taken off the track to the inside so that the horse's body is at an angle of about 35° to the long side of the manège (Fig. 7). The beauty of this exercise is that it can be started from the circle, with which both horse and trainer are now familiar, and after two or three paces in lateral movement we can return to the circle. A further advantage is that the trainer can modify the angle of the horse's body according to his ability. On a large circle we can, for instance, start to accomplish a shallow shoulder-in, with the horse nicely in balanced trot (Fig. 8). The best place to attempt the first few steps is as we arrive on the long side. The inside hand maintains the bend of the circle, the outside hand resists and controls the forward movement, the inside leg, vigorously applied at the girth, sends the horse laterally sideways, the outside leg just

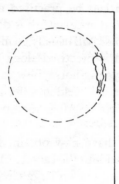

Fig. 8 A shallow shoulder-in can be performed from a large circle.

behind the girth helps to maintain impulsion. One or two paces only should be tried at first, then the horse should be sent forward onto the same-sized circle. The trainer should feel that he is pushing his inside leg towards his outside hand; that is, his right leg to left hand on a right shoulder-in, and vice versa. Should any loss of energy or rhythm occur the horse must be sent forward onto the circle again. With some impulsive horses it is often a good thing to explain this exercise at a walk, but to gain most benefit it must be perfected at the trot.

Always start with a shallow movement, the neck never bent more than the body. In the final classical movement of shoulder-in the curve of the horse's body should be equivalent to the arc of the volte, a circle of 3 metres radius, which is the smallest circle a horse can perform. Done well, without forcing, this exercise has many advantages. It develops flexibility and suppleness of back and loins; it increases the activity of the hindquarters; it frees the shoulders and lightens the forehand. In my opinion there is no need for the jumper to receive any further training in lateral movement, provided that the shoulder-in can be practised and perfected. Quite often it will be found that this work is done with better results in the open. The horse will usually go more freely outside, and if the shoulder-in is practised along the line of a hedge on the way home the young horse, now eager to please and to get back to his stable, will seldom offer any resistance. Do remember, however, to lengthen the stride once the exercise is completed.

The flexibility and suppleness we have now obtained at the trot should gradually be introduced into the canter. Most of our cantering so far has been carried out on large circles, on which the horse has learned to strike off smoothly and quietly on either leg, on the right or left circle. Now we can begin to leave the circle by going off at a tangent on a straight line, returning to the circle after a dozen strides on the straight. When this can be done on both reins, begin to lengthen the stride on the straight and ask for it to shorten as you go back to the circle. This shortening must be done with care. With the horse flexed towards the inside leg the trainer should resist with the outside hand, an action that will encourage the horse to stay on the bit when the stride shortens. The danger signal is when the horse raises his head to evade the movement. There should be no change in the head carriage – if there is the trainer has asked too much, and he must try again with greater tact.

Slow canter work over undulating ground, with the rider's seat out of the saddle about an inch, is excellent for calming and suppling. With the trainer riding in this position the horse will be encouraged to swing his quarters under him and to go frankly on to the bit.

The jumper must eventually be able to change legs smoothly and at speed, so now is the time to teach the simple

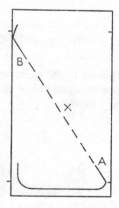

Fig. 9 Exercise in introducing the change of leg at canter. Canter left to A – make transition to trot through X to B – Canter right at B.

change through the trot. The easiest way to introduce this exercise is on a large figure of eight, asking the horse to go from canter to balanced trot and then to strike off on the other leg. If transitions from trot to canter and back have been practised, this should present no difficulty; but any new exercise must be made as simple as possible, or we will confuse and upset the horse. We therefore proceed as shown in Fig. 9. We canter left from the corner, and as soon as the horse is on the incline we reduce to trot. We are now left with plenty of room to balance and position the horse to the right

43

before striking off with the right foreleg leading. As the horse becomes more obedient and begins to understand the movement, the distance between A and B can be narrowed until we need only one trot stride and, ideally, one walk stride between each canter. This takes time and patience. Eventually it must be practised on the circle as shown in Fig. 10, the distance between A and B being reduced gradually to one stride.

An excellent suppling, balancing and obedience exercise that can be practised at this stage is the counter-canter,

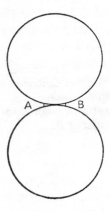

Fig. 10 Figure 8 at the canter. The distance between A and B can gradually be reduced to one stride.

which will have the effect of lengthening and lowering the stride. The counter-canter is performed when the horse leads with the right fore on the circle left, and vice versa, and he will need plenty of room for this exercise because the first move away from the leading leg must be done gradually. Having explained the exercise to the horse on both reins, shallow loops, and eventually large circles, can be practised. To take the horse into counter-canter a tactful aid is required. Cantering to the left we maintain our aid and flexion to the left, then with a light open right rein we lead the horse off to the right, hind feet following in the track of the forefeet.

HEAD CARRIAGE – Little has been said in the foregoing chapters on this subject. Some trainers insist that a low, rounded head carriage must be developed for the jumper to achieve the best results, and examples of this low head carriage are seen in the show jumping ring. Alas, many inexpert riders attempt to produce this effect by resorting to mechanical means. I am quite certain that any attempt to force a head carriage by the use of draw reins, side reins, chambons, different types of bit, etc. can only end in dismal failure. If a horse has reasonable conformation, his head and neck must be left alone as much as possible in the early stages of training. The head and neck are the horse's balancing agents: if he wants to go forward or increase his pace he will stretch them out; if he wants to decrease pace or stop he will shorten his neck to bring his centre of gravity back, and he will accentuate these actions when working under the weight of a rider.

To teach the horse to accept the bit a light continuous contact must be maintained on the mouth, the hand always following the movement of head and neck. The young horse learns to rely on this contact and eventually he comes to accept it with confidence. Initially, the head carriage will be low and extended, but as the young horse gains strength and energy and is encouraged by the rider into engaging his hocks more actively, the head and neck will gradually be raised. Similarly, the horse's jaw is stiff to begin with, but as he gains confidence in the continuous light support of the hand it will begin to soften a little. The trainer will encourage this by flexing the muscles of the neck to right and left on turns and circles; as a result the muscles of back and loin will eventually follow suit. Finally, as the head assumes its normal

45

height, according to the horse's conformation, longitudinal suppleness will be improved by bending at the poll and flexing the lower jaw.

The difficulty for most trainers is to resist the temptation to hurry this most important phase in early training. Up to twelve months should be allowed for this natural head carriage to develop, and usually a mild, jointed snaffle is the best type of bit to use for the purpose.

Once the horse's head is correctly placed the activity of the hind legs can be increased and the greater will be the impulsion. As a result the ride will become light and active.

REIN BACK – I consider the rein back a difficult movement to teach correctly, and it should not be undertaken until the young horse is up to the leg and on the bit. With the horse at this stage of training it is, nevertheless, a valuable obedience and suppling exercise, increasing the flexibility of the loins, hips, stifle and hocks.

The movement is in two-time, the horse using the diagonals, left fore and right hind, right hind and left fore, alternately. It is essential that the horse is straight before the rein back is attempted, and it will be recognised that his weight will be transferred to the rear. The head carriage remains unaltered and the pace must be even throughout. The aids for the rein back are: from a balanced halt, squeeze with both legs into a resisting hand with the rider's weight being held slightly forward. The horse, finding that he cannot go to his front, will step back. The forward urge should always be felt, and the trainer should be able to send his horse forward at any moment. This should be a balanced light movement with the spine well arched.

If the movement is attempted too early in training, the

young horse will evade by running back or by hollowing his back, moving with short stilted steps in an effort to avoid using his quarters.

IMPROVING THE JUMPING – The horse should now be jumping with freedom and confidence over small spreads and combinations of varying distances. The approach should still be from trot with the last stride in canter. The feel the trainer should get on the approach is one of mounting impulsion. Any attempt to rush or dive onto the forehand should be met by using the trotting poles again.

We can now begin to increase the number of canter strides on the approach and gradually to raise and widen our small fences, from 2 ft. in height and a 2 ft. spread to 3 ft. high with a 4 ft. spread. A guard rail should be used at most fences to help the horse in measuring distances. These slightly bigger fences and the increased impulsion that will be necessary to jump them cleanly will produce a stronger action in the horse; greater effort will be made and his back will be more rounded.

It would be as well at this point to study the action of the horse over fences and to see how the rider's body and hands must conform to this movement, allowing complete freedom of the head and neck and doing nothing to upset his balance.

During the approach the horse extends his head and neck slightly down and forward to enable him to use his hindquarters and to measure his stride. The rider must allow this movement but still hold the impulsion in his hand by maintaining contact. The rider's shoulders on the approach will be in front of the hips, seat bones in the saddle, legs close to his horse's sides.

On take-off the horse shortens his neck and raises the forehand, at the same time bringing his quarters well under him.

He then thrusts forwards and upwards. The rider's hand maintains contact, coming back towards the body a little, but to keep in balance the body must go forward. To do this the angle between body and thigh closes a fraction of a second before take-off. On topping the fence the horse stretches his head and neck forward and downwards, rounding his back with the legs tucked well underneath him. The rider's hand follows this forward reach, the shoulders go forward, and the angle between body and thigh closes until the spine is on a parallel with the line of flight of the horse. A straight line should be kept from the rider's elbow, through his little finger, along the rein to the bit.

On landing, the horse lifts his head slightly to take the weight onto the forehand. As his forelegs touch the ground the horse stretches his head and neck forward to continue his canter or gallop. The rider's hand maintains contact, his knee and ankle absorb the shock of landing and the body angle opens. Throughout the jump the rider should look up and well ahead.

This action of horse and rider obviously varies with the size of the fence and the speed of approach, and the rider must conform accordingly, the principle being to reduce to the minimum the movement necessary to stay in balance. Throughout the jump the rider's weight should sink into his heel, and his lower leg should press against his horse's sides close to the girth, encouraging the horse forward in rhythm with the stride. There must be no thumping with the heels; lightness must always be aimed for in the application of the aid.

To improve the harmonic use of the leg and to give confidence to horse and rider a distance rail can be used. Cavalletti placed at varying distances from the main fences will enable the trainer to shorten or lengthen strides at will. Some of these distances have already been used in our early training, but although the length of stride varies considerably with the speed and the type of fence being jumped, a distance of 45 ft. between a cavalletto and a 3 ft. fence of double rails will give three reasonable strides. The rider can practise using his legs in rhythm very easily at this particular distance, and with experience the number of strides can be altered, and lengthened or shortened, according to how the horse is jumping. Soon both horse and trainer will begin to see their stride and then the distance rail can be removed. With practice, over a small fence of the type described, the rider will learn whether he is going to meet the fence correctly or not and will quite quickly acquire the knack of shortening or lengthening the stride to remedy any situation that might arise. Nevertheless, alterations in the stride should be made smoothly and as far away from the fence as possible. In fact, of course, at this early stage in jumping training it is better to leave the young horse alone and let him find his own stride. If the schooling, jumping loose and from the trot, has been correct it is enough for the rider to bring his horse into the zone of take-off well balanced and with sufficient impulsion to clear the fence. Attempting to place a young horse at this stage of training will rob him of the initiative we have been trying to build up.

Chapter 4

FURTHER STEPS IN JUMPING

ZONE OF TAKE-OFF – In front of every fence there is a zone from which a horse can jump and clear his fence with the minimum of effort. This zone alters according to the height and width of the fence (Fig. 11). Take, for example, an

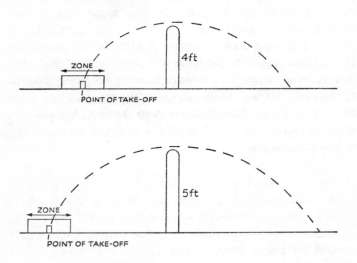

Fig. 11 Zone of take-off. The point of take-off with a 4-ft. fence is about 1⅓ times the height of the fence away.

upright fence 4 ft. high. The best point of take-off to clear the fence is about $1\frac{1}{3}$ times the height of the fence away, depending on the speed of approach. This is not to say that this is the *only* point from which the fence can be successfully jumped, as any horse with reasonable scope can still clear it even if he comes closer in or stands further off; but it remains the ideal point of take-off. It will be appreciated that as the fence gets higher or wider the take-off zone will become narrower and greater accuracy in the approach will be necessary.

Depending on the horse's scope, ability and state of training he should jump most fences of 4 ft. and a normal spread without being 'placed'. Water presents a different problem and will be discussed later. Remember that too much precision schooling will make the horse bored and may turn him sour. The work on the flat and over fences that we have been discussing must be alternated with work across country to keep him happy and interested. Riding over undulating and broken ground, jumping small obstacles, up and down hill, tackling ditches, small walls, post and rails, and so on, in the open country all provide variety and experience. Jump these little natural fences from a slow trot or canter, keep the horse calm, don't overface him and remember to reward him with a pat when he has done well.

JUMPING A SMALL COURSE – Jumping a series of fences involving changes of direction is the next step. The height of these fences should remain low and they should incorporate spreads as much as possible. Only four or five fences will be needed for a first practice, and they should be fences with which the horse is already familiar. Our aim is to ride smoothly and quietly between fences and on the approach to each one. We do not want the horse to show any excitement, nor do we want him to hot up, and to avoid these undesirable tendencies, we must make no sudden changes in pace or direction. Place the fences so that they can be negotiated on a simple figure-of-eight course with easy turns and plenty of room between each jump. Most horses tend to loose impulsion on turns and on being asked for a decrease of pace, so the trainer's primary job is to concentrate on maintaining the pace through the turn by using a strong inside leg, and it is now that we shall appreciate the benefit of our earlier schooling on the flat. Decreases of pace must be made slowly, with the rider's seat bones held deep in the saddle and the body assuming a more upright position. The first attempts at jumping these small courses will be done mainly in trot, using this pace between fences and on the turns and allowing a few strides in canter before each fence. The number of strides depends on the natural impulsion of the horse. If he is the type that is over-impulsive one must keep him trotting much longer; in fact, with some excitable horses one should reduce to a walk between fences to curb their excitement. With those of a calmer temperament it may be necessary to encourage them to take three or four canter strides before each fence. If various types of course can be jumped in this manner over a period of two or three months the calmness brought about by the early training will continue and many bad habits will be avoided from the outset.

At this early stage always:
Ride straight before and after each fence;
Control the pace and maintain balance and impulsion;
Turn correctly;
Avoid refusals;
Remember that accuracy in your work on the flat is essential.

All work over fences must be preceded by suppling and obedience exercises on the flat if it is to be successful and performed in a state of calm. Before putting a horse at any fence the trainer should feel that his horse is between hand and leg; ready to move impulsively forward or to come back to hand calmly and without fuss. To this end, the exercises discussed in earlier chapters must be practised regularly and should be increased in difficulty as training progresses.

The trot is the schooling pace and the one employed in our earlier training over fences, but the normal paces from which to jump are the canter and the gallop, and so our training must now be aimed at obtaining maximum control and complete flexibility at these paces. Let us consider the various exercises on the flat and over fences that will help us to achieve this objective. One may say that such exercises are only applicable to the specialised skills of the show jumper, but by teaching the young horse to jump accurately and smoothly over a variety of small courses we shall be improving his ability to perform creditably in the hunting field and across country.

To jump in canter the trainer must continue to practise striking off with the correct leg leading from trot and eventually from walk. It is essential that the horse should strike off freely on either leg without favouring a certain lead as is the case with so many badly-trained animals. Frequent transitions from walk to canter and from canter to walk will help, and will also improve the balanced canter. At first the horse will make one or two strides at the trot before striking off, but he will soon learn to go straight from walk to canter and vice versa. This exercise should be practised on the incline and on the circle, great care being taken to allow the swing of the head in the first stride of canter, with the rider's hand following the mouth without imposing any restriction.

A simple study of the footfalls at the canter is a help in obtaining strike-offs from the walk easily and smoothly. We have already noted that the canter is a pace of three-time. The sequence of footfalls are as follows. To canter with the right lead: first movement is near hind; then off hind and near fore together; followed by off fore. A period of suspension is then apparent, when all four legs are off the ground, following which the sequence starts again. To obtain a smooth transition from walk to canter the aid must be applied as the desired hind leg is coming to the ground. With a little study and practice most horsemen can achieve this and will soon learn to feel when that hind leg comes down. The transition from canter to walk can be made only at the end of the stride, therefore the aid to walk is applied as the leading foreleg is coming to the ground. This movement can, in fact,

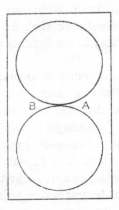

Fig. 12 The figures used to teach the simple changes from walk to canter.

be seen and should eventually be felt. Whenever the aid is applied the rider must make certain he is sitting square in the saddle, with his weight evenly distributed over both seat bones; this applies particularly to the canter aids, when any

incorrect posture of the body will affect the horse's balance
and consequently his ability to obey our commands.

Practise the simple changes through the walk, gradually
decreasing the number of strides between each lead, and
then start to teach the simple change out of the circle until it
can be done with only a few paces in the walk (Fig. 12). The
size of circles at the canter can now be gradually reduced until
at a collected canter of a 10 metre diameter is achieved. This
exercise should be alternated with lengthened strides down

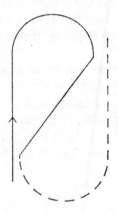

Fig. 13 An exercise in counter-
canter. The unbroken line
represents true canter, the
broken one the maintenance of
the same lead in counter-canter.

the long side. At this stage, the rider should also increase the
difficulty of the counter-canter work as shown in Fig. 13.
Shallow serpentines can be practised in canter until large
circles can be carried out completely in counter-canter, with
the horse correctly flexed towards the leading leg. These
exercises will help to cadence the canter and to increase
suppleness and agility; they will also help to put the horse
on the bit and to secure implicit obedience. This work leads
up to flying changes of leg, where the horse changes legs at
the moment of suspension without relapsing into trot; but

to obtain such changes smoothly and without excitement takes a great deal of preparation.

Do not do too much of this work at any one time. The counter-canter is difficult for the young horse, and he will tend to increase his pace to maintain balance at first, but as he becomes more supple the trainer will learn to balance him just as he does in the true canter. Give frequent rests at a long rein walk during the schooling sessions, because these exercises are very tiring, particularly for the neck and loin muscles. Never, never punish the horse for a disobedience. Repetition is the only cure for this, and the trainer must look to his application of aids before blaming the horse. Above all, keep your horse *calm*.

Concurrently with work on the flat we can begin to alter our approach to a fence. So far the approach has always been well prepared and straight, and on landing we have always gone straight for at least three strides. Now, however, we have reached a stage where we can think about introducing various methods designed to develop the horse's initiative when jumping.

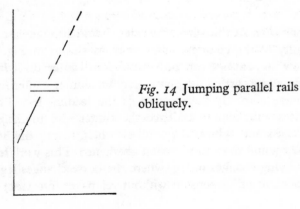

Fig. 14 Jumping parallel rails obliquely.

JUMPING EXERCISES – To gain valuable seconds in a show jumping competition it is often necessary to jump from an angle. Over low fences this lesson can easily be taught because the take-off zone is wide and not too demanding, but over bigger fences, 4 ft. and over, the zone becomes narrower and the horse must therefore learn to adjust his stride. The exercise is best done over low parallel rails, from a walk to a walk (Fig. 14). The horse can first be inclined from the track three or more strides from the fence, with the

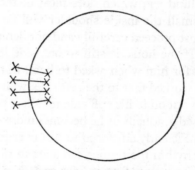

Fig. 15 Trotting cavalletti on the circle. The inside distance is 4 ft. apart, the outside 5–6 ft.

strides gradually being reduced to two. Jumping slowly at an angle teaches both horse and rider to judge distances, and it also makes the young horse very agile. It goes without saying that the trainer's body must be well forward and very supple on take-off, the hand allowing all the rein that is needed.

The exercise is also very useful for a horse that persistently runs out to one side. Ideally, of course, a horse should never run out, but when this evasion does occur this is one way of keeping control into the fence of a horse that falls onto one shoulder. For the horse that runs out to the right, for instance, the approach is made obliquely from the right of the fence.

Jumping on the circle is also a valuable gymnastic exercise; it can be introduced initially by practising on a circle of cavalletti. The cavalletti should be placed on a 20-metre circle (as shown in Fig. 15), 4 ft. apart on the inside and 5 to 6 ft. on the outside. Start at a walk, increasing to a good rhythmic trot only when the horse is quite calm. This exercise demands a great deal of the horse, and particularly of his inside hind leg, which does most of the work: if the circle is too small the inside shoulder will be cramped. So the trainer must proceed carefully and not demand too much of his pupil. If the horse is stiff to one side it will be even more difficult for him when asked to bend in that direction. He should be worked first to the soft side, which is easier for him, and then put on to his stiff side for short periods, which can be increased gradually as he becomes more supple. When the horse is sufficiently advanced to trot over four low cavalletti in good rhythm the trainer can start to ride over raised cavalletti on the curve, first in trot and then with the last two strides in canter. This leads us on to our next exercise.

It will be noticed that when jumping on the curve the horse, if well balanced on the approach, will land with the inside leg leading. This important fact will enable the trainer to influence his horse as he tops the fence and encourage him to land with the correct leg leading when a change of direction is required. Our next exercise is jumping on a figure of eight (Fig. 16).

Use crossed rails about 2 ft. high and have the cross exactly where the horse changes rein out of the circle. Work first at balanced trot over this fence. The young horse will invariably land in a canter stride. Practise three or four times to the right and then the same to the left; then alternate with a varying number of times to both sides. As the horse becomes more obedient in this exercise so will his canter on landing be more relaxed and easy. The trainer can then start to canter on the approach, and the change in the air will be achieved. This, is not, of course, the orthodox way of teaching a horse the flying change; it is really a more advanced exercise in obedience and agility.

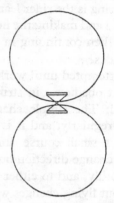

Fig. 16 Jumping cross-rails on a figure 8.

Jumping on the circle will very quickly bring out any stiffness or resistance to one side that the young horse may still have. He should at this stage accept the rein equally on both sides, but some young horses who are very stiff take a long time before they are even to right and to left. Should the horse still be stiff to one side he will fall in on the circle or veer out, and to overcome this more work must be done on a larger circle until his suppleness is increased. In addition, the exercises at counter-canter and shoulder-in can be used at this stage and are probably the best methods by which suppleness and obedience are obtained.

FLYING CHANGE – To teach the young horse to execute a flying change, smoothly, in balance and on a straight line without increase of pace, is a very advanced stage of dressage training, and the nearer we can get to this with any horse so much the better. But the show jumping rider, for instance, has a great deal to think about when jumping a round, and on a change of direction his horse should ideally change the leading leg in one stride. This fluent change without loss of speed cannot be achieved without proper schooling, however. What we so often see in his jumping ring is the rider leaning forward, swinging his horse's forehand and making the horse change in front but not behind, and then continuing in this ungainly manner for the next six strides!

The flying change should not be attempted until work on the flat is well advanced and implicit obedience in striking off on either leg has been obtained. The simple change, through the trot, must be practised regularly, and it is the method always used when jumping a small course during training. When the young horse will change direction out of the circle over the crossed rails smoothly, and to either leg, is soon enough to begin thinking about flying changes when riding a course. What is wanted is a flying change in one stride that is smooth with no loss of speed.

There are various ways to teach the young horse to carry out this important movement, but whichever one the trainer uses he must remember the following points. There is only one time during the canter stride that the horse can make a clean change, and that is at the end of a stride, during the period of suspension. The period of suspension takes place immediately after the leading foreleg comes to the ground, which is the end of the stride. The trainer must therefore apply his aid for the change as this leading foreleg comes down. This gives the average horse time to react and to start the change of leg behind in the first time of the next stride, which will ensure a smooth and fluent change. The change starts from behind, therefore the trainer must sit on his seat when applying the aid, and not lean forward and attempt to swing his horse into changing. This amateurish method only weights the forehand and frees the quarters just at the wrong moment. When applying the aids to change try to have the young horse as straight as possible. This makes the change easier for him and therefore more fluent. The simplest aid for the change is the diagonal aid used for the normal strike-off. The main difficulty experienced by most young riders is the timing of the aid and the smoothness in its application. The rider has learnt to position his horse at walk and trot by changing his aids; he must also learn to do this in canter before he can execute a smooth flying change. The best method is to practise this on the incline across the manège as we did in the simple change, asking for one or two trot strides. Finally, one can eliminate the trot stride. Quietly straighten your horse as you pass across the centre and apply the aid for the opposite leg just before reaching the track. The best way of timing the aid is to count the rhythm: 1-2-3, 1-2-3-change-1-2-3. The rider must sit as still as possible, with his weight even on both seat bones, although the tendency is to put the weight to the inside. Any confusion can only be caused by the rider, so if the horse becomes upset and excited he must be brought back to a loose rein walk and calmed before trying again. When the change can be carried out fluently on both reins in this manner, then it should be practised out of the circle.

Eventually the jumper, particularly the show jumper, must learn to change on his own on a change of direction when galloping on. This he will find easy to do, and the trainer's aids can become lighter and lighter. But to teach the flying change from the aids ensures a clean change in one stride.

SEEING YOUR STRIDE – The horse and trainer gain confidence in each other, their boldness in riding into fences will increase. If all fences are kept small and have a solid appearance our young horse should jump cleanly both from trot and canter. Jumping from trot teaches the horse to approach without rushing, and to round his back. It also has the added advantage that he cannot arrive in the take-off zone on a half stride; he is always right for his fence. In canter and gallop the stride is longer, and very often the horse takes off too close or too far back. As we have already said, over fences up to 4 ft. the average good horse can cope, but as jumping develops and fences get bigger and wider, the trainer must develop his judgement of distance so that he can help his horse where necessary to arrive in the zone of take-off. The point of take-off is where the horse puts his leading foreleg on the last canter or gallop stride before jumping. And to see this point and adjust the horse's stride some four or five strides away needs a great deal of practice and skill. Jumping cavalletti at various distances helps a lot to cultivate one's judgement, but the problem is much more difficult at the faster paces.

The best method is to use the distance rail placed at a suitable distance from various fences to give a number of non-jumping strides. Use two fences for this practice, one upright fence with a ground line, and the other parallel rails without a ground line, with both fences about 3 ft. 6 in. high to begin with and the parallel with a spread of 3 ft. It must be remembered that the length of the horse's stride varies with the distance between obstacles and that such variations will be exaggerated by any departure from an even speed. If you allow 11 ft. for each stride and 12 ft. for take-off and landing, you can pace out approximate three-stride and four-stride distances. Place your schooling fences as shown in

Fig. 17, and place turning markers of small oil drums some distance from each fence so that you ride straight before and after. The distance between cavalletti and upright fence should give three strides, and it should give four strides to the parallel. Now the trainer must approach with an even

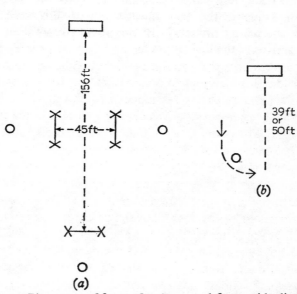

Fig. 17a Placement of fences for three- and four-stride distances.

Fig. 17b Another method of training the eye to assess distances and strides accurately by using a turning marker in front of the fence.

canter stride looking at the fence and not the distance rail. As he lands over the rail he must count his stride to the point of take-off for the following fence. Practise this regularly, and then pull the distance rail to one side and try adjusting the stride without the distance rail.

Another good method of training the eye for distance is shown in the second diagram of Fig. 17. The marker shown is a turning marker. Walk towards the marker, and as you turn round it put the horse into canter; you will then have three or four strides before take-off. If both these methods are practised regularly one can soon learn to see the stride at these distances, and for the average rider this is good enough. Adjusting the stride must be practised by lengthening or shortening the stride to suit these distances as the horse arrives at the distance rail.

Chapter 5

SHOW JUMPING

In the more specialised and expert world of show jumping developing the eye and adjusting distances becomes a much more exact affair. The problems that are set by a well-built and well-planned course are many: problems of height and shape of each fence; problems of distance between each fence; and finally speed. Let us consider each in turn. Fences can be classified under four headings: vertical or upright; parallels with or without a ground line; staircase or triple rail type; pyramid, as in a hogsback; and on its own, the fence with width and no height – water. Height in relation to design is vital; a single rail with no ground line at 4 ft. high would be virtually unjumpable to a novice horse, but a staircase at 4 ft. 6 in. would cause no problem.

The trainer must provide himself with examples of each type of fence, solidly made but adjustable, and the young horse must be encouraged to jump boldly over small examples of each, first as individual fences and then as a small course. Verticals, in the early stages, must always have a well-defined ground line, preferably starting with a pole some distance from the base of the vertical, because most young horses make the mistake of getting too close to upright fences. As he gains experience the pole can be moved closer to the base. Parallel rails should also have a ground line to begin with, with the gap between well filled in. When training over this type of fence always go for spread before height. The staircase can be a most inviting fence when built simply, with the first step low to the ground and with each ascending part a proportional distance higher and more spread away. It can be made more difficult by accentuating the angle of ascent and by narrowing the spread between each pole. The pyramid presents much the same problem. If the horse takes off in the right place and clears the top pole his natural line of descent will take him clear of the further poles.

As I have mentioned in previous chapters, to the horse with scope the take-off zone can be very elastic with fences up to 4 ft. high, but as fences get higher and wider the problem of take-off and getaway on landing becomes increasingly difficult. For example, the vertical fence allows for the greatest margin of error, the take-off being well back or close to, but if take-off is too close the angle of descent will be very steep and will interfere with a fluent getaway on landing. Spreads with height require great accuracy in the adjustment of stride, and very often the background of early training in jumping loose adds boldness and scope over this type of fence.

Water in show jumping has often been a bogey to many competitors. The first essential to remember when schooling over water is that the horse must remain balanced. Riding a horse at speed into a water jump so that he is driven onto his forehand is courting disaster. A lengthening of the stride is essential, but impulsion and balance must be maintained as in a spread with height. The take-off zone at water is difficult to judge as there is only a small brush fence placed in front as a guide. In schooling over water, the problem is to get the horse to take off as close to the brush fence as possible, and to jump with a lengthening stride, gaining height above the water. This can be done by positioning the distance rail four long strides away, and by placing a light rail one foot higher than, and two feet beyond, the brush fence; this distance being gradually increased to about four feet. This method, when carried out with patience, is very effective.

So much for the height and shape of obstacles; but show jumping today is not just a matter of jumping a number of large fences. A well-designed course – and most are – must be ridden as one fluent whole; this calls for good judgement of pace and distance by the rider and instant and smooth obedience from the horse. A horse's stride varies considerably, depending on his speed and impulsion, and the course builder takes this very much into consideration when planning his courses. Distances between fences can be easy or difficult, and a rider must have a thorough knowledge of these distances so that the young horse can be schooled to meet both.

In any given course, fences that are more than 80 ft. apart can be classed as unrelated. The distance is great enough for the adjustment of stride to be made, there being at least six strides here for the average horse. Related fences are those which are between 39 ft. 4 in. and 80 ft. apart. Below 39 ft. 4 in. fences are classed as combinations and must be jumped together. Until the young horse has built up his confidence we should always school over correct and easy distances. With the average horse and with fences up to 4 ft. high, 24 ft. between two vertical fences will give one non-jumping stride, and 33 ft. will give two strides. When jumping from a vertical to a spread the distance should be shortened by 6–12 in., depending on the spread; when jumping from a spread to a vertical the distance should be lengthened to 25 ft. for one non-jumping stride, or 35 ft. for two strides, because of the angle of descent over the first fence. When jumping a combination of two spreads the distance for two verticals would be correct. Difficult distances in a one-stride combination could be 23 ft. or less, calling for a short stride, or 29 ft. 6 in., calling for two short strides or one very long one. In a two-stride combination anything less than 33 ft. calls for two short strides, and the maximum distance of 39 ft. 4 in. means two long or three short strides. Measurements are from the inside to inside of each fence.

Each of these problems requires a different approach to the first fence. In the first case a short-striding approach is necessary, and in the second case a long stride is called for. Loss of balance and impulsion is the danger here. Practice over related fences up to 80 ft. apart requires much more judgement of pace by the rider, who should endeavour always to get cleanly away on landing and to maintain a smooth even stride between fences. Again, first practise easy distances, and try the difficult ones only when real confidence has been achieved.

The greater the distance between fences the greater will be the increase in the horse's length of stride; the average of 11 ft. may indeed go up to 14 or 15 ft. in top-class show jumpers. For the purposes of training, however, the following distances usually make easy non-jumping strides: 45 ft., 56 ft., 67 ft., for 3, 4 and 5 strides respectively. Some adjustment is usually necessary, depending on the horse.

Jumping fences on a straight line at these distances helps to develop the eye and gives both horse and rider confidence. Only in the top flight of jumping competitions do we see difficult distances produced in a combination. All novice competitions and Foxhunter classes should place doubles and trebles at suitable distances, but with related fences there are often difficult distances. A difficult distance is one where the horse meets the fence on a half stride, and to meet it correctly

68

an adjustment must be made at least three strides away, and preferably further away than that. Any adjustment in stride must be made as far back as possible, because any interference during the last three strides will cause either loss of balance or loss of impulsion, and, if persisted in, will lead to a loss of confidence and refusals. Whether the stride is lengthened or shortened depends very much on the temperament and balance of the horse, but both should be practised. Here are two examples of difficult distances and how to tackle them. Three-and-a-half strides can be tricky, so place the distance rail at 48 ft. from the practice fence. Try jumping it in two ways: first by approaching the first fence strongly, jumping out over it and coming into the second fence with long strides. If your horse jumps in three strides rounding his back this is the answer for him; if he flattens or puts in a short one, then try the second method of approach. Come into the first fence with a shortened stride and jump your second fence with four short non-jumping strides.

The second distance to practise this exercise over is 69 ft. If your horse has plenty of scope and is naturally well balanced, lengthening the stride is to be recommended. If he is inclined to flatten or go on his forehand, a quick half-stride immediately after the first fence will usually bring him right for the second.

The next thing the rider has to contend with is maintaining the pace when changing direction. Turns should be made wide to begin with, but they must always be accurate, with speed, impulsion and balance being maintained. As the horse improves in suppleness and agility, much tighter turns can be made, but success in accurate and speedy changes of direction depends on your training on the flat. The rider should feel that his horse is always well between hand and leg, ready to shoot forward to the lightest pressure of the leg, and to obey instantly any indication from the hand. Violent rein aids unsupported by the leg only cause loss of impulsion and fluency.

Work at the trot is a basic essential in training, as we have seen, but the show jumper's pace is canter and gallop, and flexibility and calm obedience must therefore be practised at these gaits. Lengthening and shortening the stride on circles and on straight lines provides a sound base from which to work, as does the spiral at the canter, shortening the stride as the circle gets smaller, and lengthening it to increase the size. Flying changes on a change of direction should be second nature to the accomplished show jumper, and they should be carried out without loss of speed and without the horse becoming disunited.

Unfortunately, many horses are ruined by being taken into competitions before they are ready. The standard of show jumping today is high, and if one is to succeed, as much work as possible must be done over small courses of varying types before entering the ring. A horse's first competition should be well within his jumping capacity, and it is often good practice to introduce young jumpers to the show ring by entering them in a hunter class so that they can get used to the atmosphere. Many professionals take young horses to shows three and four times without jumping them. Having decided on your competition, get to the showground in good time, so that your horse can get over the first excitement and settle down. This will also give you time to study the course. Pace your distances between combinations and related fences; decide where you are going to turn and how you will approach each fence. Go through each fence in your mind without looking at the course; this is the best way to remember it. If you are fortunate enough not to go first, watch other riders and see where the difficulties lie. Have your horse warm, supple and attentive by quietly working him in, and keep a rug on him if it is cold. Jump the practice fence two or three times immediately before entering the arena, but don't overdo it; you want your horse 'fresh on his legs, but cool in his head'. Walk into the arena, going close to the fences you pass on your way to salute the judges, if it is appropriate. If your first fence is right-handed, make certain that your circle is the same. Canter on a large circle when the bell goes and try to adopt immediately the normal schooling pace you use at home. Do your best to keep that pace even throughout the course, making no violent alterations in speed but just moving forward with good balance and impulsion. This is the rider's main task, to guide, control and balance, so that the approach to each fence is as smooth as possible. As I have mentioned earlier, with fences at novice height there is little need to place your horse; the more he is left alone, the better he will jump.

You want your horse's first experience in the show ring to be a pleasant one, and not associated with whip, spur and the rattling of poles. If your horse refuses he has either been surprised by something he has not seen before or confused by the mass of poles beyond the fence. Treat the whole matter quietly and try again, approaching the second time from a slightly different angle and a little slower. If your horse is a consistent refuser, he shouldn't be in the ring; the root of most refusals is in the training, and it should be tackled at home. Having completed the course and crossed the finish line, return to a long rein walk and leave the arena at this pace. The conscientious rider will then analyse his round, jumping each fence again and deciding where he and his horse could have improved the performance, and where more training is needed, either on the flat or with the actual take-off and getaway. The next few competitions should be tackled on these lines, getting the horse to jump in the pace he likes best, without fuss or hurry. If the young horse has the will to do it his natural ability will begin to develop, and you will know whether you have a potential high-class show jumper or not. If he is jumping well in the ring the amount of jumping he does in training need be very little. In fact, older horses are rarely jumped outside the arena during the season, though a young horse's training must continue of course, but mostly on the flat, with the occasional medium-sized fence or combination. The aim is to perfect his obedience and suppleness, not to wear him out by trying to jump big fences.

Developing speed on a course is a prime consideration, but the trainer should consider this only when the young horse has jumped a number of novice competitions at a balanced pace with as little fluctuation in stride as possible. Speed is achieved first by lengthening the stride, and not by increasing the number of strides. Watch any racehorse being ridden in a finish, if the lengthening is done carefully the balance will always be maintained. If he arrives at the point of take-off with the stride too extended he will jump flat and the parabola will not be as well-rounded as is required for show fences. The next point to consider in riding against the clock is the track to be taken. Every corner must be cut short and must be ridden at speed. One must accelerate through the corners, and this is where good schooling on the flat and instant obedience to the inside leg will gain its due reward. To cut corners, fences must necessarily be jumped at an angle; and as the horse tops the fence, the skilful horseman will determine the change of direction. But the round must remain fluent, or more time will be lost than gained. In addition, violent changes of pace and direction will tire your horse out. Very few competitions are won today on the first round, and the horse who performs smoothly and with fluency will be saving energy for the jump-off.

The number of shows that the young horse should be taken to in his first season must depend very much on his general fitness, his age, his legs and the state of the going. But a maximum of eight shows should not be exceeded; otherwise there is a risk of injury or staleness. Constant attention must be paid to overall fitness. If a horse suddenly loses form there is a reason for it, and it is usually connected with soreness, stiffness of muscles, corns, slight sprains, etc. A shoe, slightly twisted, can pass unnoticed, but can cause a horse discomfort and a loss of form. Good management is essential to correct feeding, watering and exercise, but when a horse does go off form, the best remedy is a rest from jumping. Staleness often first manifests itself in refusals, and if this occurs in the consistent jumper then a searching examination into the cause must be made. If refusing occurs during training, although the horse is completely sound, there is something faulty in the trainer or the riding. The reason may be psychological or physical, and the good trainer will, with patience and commonsense, find it. If training has been sound and progressive, horses with a normal temperament do not refuse unless they are overfaced, sickened by too much jumping or over-fresh. The remedy in each case is obvious and can soon be put right by a trainer of experience. Other reasons could be bad bitting, and the pain and fear caused by it or a badly-fitting saddle. Not nearly enough attention is paid to saddle fitting. There are far too many saddles that are too low on the withers and too narrow in the gullet to take the width of the backbone. It could be lack of nerve, or incompetence, on the part of the rider. The horse is invariably blamed by this type of rider, and it needs a trainer on the ground to put the rider right.

F

73

Whatever the cause, patience, followed by quiet but firm riding over small obstacles, will usually improve matters. Work on the flat to re-establish obedience to hand and leg is essential, and often a short period of loose jumping will help to restore lost confidence. In training, refusals must be avoided at all costs, which is why a gradual build up of the horse's confidence must be achieved by a sound and progressive system. Once a horse starts to refuse in the show ring it takes a long time to put the matter right, and it is very often the beginning of the end for that horse as a show jumper.

In the show ring you are jumping in front of a very critical audience; they may be uninformed but they pay to see a good performance. The good show jumper produces this by having himself and his horse fit and well trained up to the standard of the particular show. The rider who turns himself and his horse out well, and who jumps in good style, will always be popular with the crowd.

Good show jumps are very expensive items to buy, but a necessary minimum must always be available for training. Six well-made cavalletti are a must; so much can be done with them in building fences easily and quickly, but any material used must be solid and safe. Poles should be at least 4 in. in diameter; made-up stands must be firm enough to withstand a hard knock. In fact, at least four fences built to BSJA specifications are a good buy. A number of solid fences made from sleepers, telegraph poles, etc., are excellent for schooling. They should look and be solid but they must not be big; fences that can be increased to 3 ft. high and 3 ft. wide are quite sufficient in size. Your aim is to obtain maximum obedience from your horse, not to be continually testing his jumping ability. Site your schooling fences so that they can present a variety of problems, and if you can persuade other people to build small courses for you so much the better. Jump the young horse over other training courses when possible. The occasional half-day's hunting later in his training will teach him to look after himself, and to go quietly in company and in more exciting surroundings and it will do nothing but good.

Finally, it takes as much time to make a show jumper as it does to train a horse for any other purpose. A man recently said to me: 'This dressage is all very well, but it takes such a long time. It takes five years and more to produce a horse to Olympic standard!' I may say it takes this amount of time to produce an Olympic show jumper, and any trainer who tries to produce show jumpers in a year ruins more horses than he makes.

Chapter 6

HUNTING

It has been said that the only work from which a horse derives pleasure and in which he takes a personal interest is foxhunting. I do not wholly agree with this, but I do know that some of the worst rides I have had in my life were on horses that had not been properly prepared for hunting, and if young horses are properly schooled and prepared then most of them, whatever their job in life, are usually improved by the occasional day with hounds.

In the preceding chapters we have gone through a basic system of schooling on the flat and over fences that will produce in about one year a horse that is obedient and well balanced, that goes freely forward between hand and leg at the basic paces, and that will jump a variety of fences from trot and canter, over both natural and made fences. Let us suppose the young horse's mounted schooling started in March. By October it should be possible to take him cub-hunting, so that he may see hounds and begin his education as a hunter the right way. The excitement of seeing hounds for the first time will often cause a young horse to lose his head and temporarily to forget all he has learned, so this first day must be approached with some care. The young horse should be well worked the previous day, and on the cub-hunting morning should be hacked at least the last four miles

76

to the meet, in company with an old and steady hunter if this is possible. Make certain that you arrive early, so that your young horse can watch others arrive in their ones and twos. Let him look on from some distance away, not too close to hounds. When hounds move off, walk your horse quietly away in the opposite direction! Never follow behind an exciting jostling crowd, there is nothing more likely to cause your horse to 'hot up'. If it is possible, circle round for a mile or so and return quietly to within some distance of the covertside.

This form of training should be done often during October and November; allow him to mingle with other horses but stay wide of hounds. He must realise that implicit obedience is still essential, and this will only be achieved if the horse is calm. The excitement of the first real hunt should not be experienced until the trainer is absolutely sure of his young horse's temperament, and then it should be tackled sensibly. By late January he should be well enough schooled, and fit enough, to have a short day up with hounds. Jumping across country in company with other horses is bound to be exciting, so he must be kept well in hand and not allowed to gallop on, which is something he has not really learned to do yet. He must be steadied at his fences and trotted down steep slopes. Many fences out hunting are best jumped from a trot and here his early training will stand him in good stead. Be careful not to overtax your horse, two half-days a week are tremendous fun and good value; one long day which exhausts your horse can do great harm both mentally and physically. Education continues in the hunting field, and such things as the practical application of turning on the forehand will now be discovered when opening gates, as well as the obedience to hand and leg when turning quietly away from the body of the hunt and the accuracy required on the approach to the part of the fence you have selected to jump. The good trainer carries on this work for many weeks. Great tact and much guile is necessary during this important phase of training. Because the young horse is excited by hounds, much greater energy and impulsion is created; this must be guided in the right channels so that mind and muscle continue to be developed and yet the young horse is not allowed to get over-excited, risking injury to his mouth, tendons and joints.

When the going is good, practise lengthening the stride into a gallop. Slow transitions are vital both for increase and decrease of pace. Care should be taken not to change the leading leg as the horse lengthens from canter into gallop. A few words to explain this pace are not out of place here. The gallop is a pace of four-time. As the horse extends from canter into gallop, the diagonals, which come to the ground together in the canter, becomes disassociated, giving the fourth beat, but there is still a period of suspension as in the canter. The inside laterals should lead, as in the canter, and a horse will change his lead in the same way.

The rider's position at gallop is most important. If the horse is going freely forward, on the bit and in front of the legs, then the seat is out of the saddle; but the knee remains supple and *sinks deeper*, the *calves* grip, and the angle of body and thigh closes. This enables the rider to stay in balance without hanging onto his horse's mouth – which is the one sure way to make a horse pull at the gallop. The horse must carry his own head but must be given the confidence of a strong even contact by a tactful hand, following the movement, and a body that is in balance without support from the reins.

In this manner we get our young horse obedient but bold calm but energetic, comfortable and accomplished.

Ideally a horse should hunt in a snaffle, but a hunter must be under control at all times, for your own safety and the safety of others, so most hunters should be trained to the double bridle. If you look upon the double bridle as a four wheel brake, then you shouldn't use it. The purpose of the curb is to teach a horse to relax his jaw and bend at the poll when the head and hocks are in the correct position, so that the rider has a lighter ride and greater control. To use a double bridle correctly a firm and independent seat is the

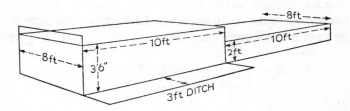

Fig. 18 Detail of a table fence.

first essential; tact and feel is the second. Used correctly and systematically, the double bridle can turn a heavy unpleasant ride into a balanced and agreeable one.

Although a hunter rarely jumps big fences, he will jump in many trappy places, at any pace from walk to gallop, never really knowing what the take-off and landing are like. So he must be sure-footed and well-balanced. A good system of schooling will always improve his ability, and the basic training over cavalletti and small solid fences is as necessary a preparation for hunting as it is for show jumping. There is one fence that can be built in the training area which I have always found teaches horses to be agile and bold, and that is a table jump (see Fig. 18). This obstacle can be made with sleepers and filled in with earth, and it can have a top layer of cinders or pea gravel. There is a ditch on one side only. The jump can be taken in a variety of ways: starting at a walk and trot over the lowest part from the side; then from the end, stepping up to the highest part and turning right or left to jump off. With practice, your horse will get progressively bolder and more agile, eventually taking it in his stride at a fast pace and from any direction.

A good hunter is a great companion, and the exhilaration of riding to hounds across good country, the satisfaction that is felt when hacking home after a good day, can only be achieved by careful and patient schooling.

Chapter 7

POINT TO POINT RIDING

Many young men and women are keen to train their own hunters for point-to-points or for a hunt steeplechase under rules. Today the point-to-point has become very professional, and to win a race one must have a very good-class horse.

There are a number of things to take into account when preparing a hunter for a point-to-point. Out hunting, your horse jumps in a collected manner, from a trot or canter, rarely at an extended gallop. In a race he must learn to jump at speed, with a flatter parabola, and to choose his point of take-off at this faster pace. Then there is the question of fitness. Towards the end of a season, if a horse has been regularly hunted, he will have worn light, and he cannot possibly be put into fast work unless he has time to build up first. The last point to consider is the fitness of the rider. We will discuss each of these points in turn.

The basic training in jumping, plus our short days in the hunting field, will have given the horse confidence over most types of fences; our aim now is to get him to jump at speed in close company. Three flights of hurdles well laced with gorse make the best schooling fences. They should be wide enough for at least two horses to jump abreast. The first flight should be well sloped, but the second and third can be made a little more upright. The keynote must always be confidence, so the horse should be jumped over the hurdles alone at a normal hunting pace to begin with. The last hurdle can then have a guard rail put some three feet in front of it. A hunter must be given time to learn to jump fast, or he will hot up and make bad mistakes. When jumping at speed he will learn to stand back, and the rider must be careful to keep his weight well over his centre of gravity and to allow complete freedom of the head and neck throughout the leap, at the same time maintaining contact. The rider will use a much shorter stirrup leather than for hunting, but he must still be capable of driving his horse into his fences when necessary. The prospective point-to-pointer should now be ridden in company, preferable with an older horse, and every effort should be made to encourage him to keep up with, and take off beside, the 'schoolmaster'. It is most important to hold your horse absolutely straight throughout and to stop any tendency to jump to one side. Some horses do this when coming wrong into a fence, and it can well develop into a habit. A horse that jumps crooked in a race is a menace. There should be a lengthening of the stride on the approach to encourage the horse to jump well out. A properly schooled horse who is a good effortless jumper will gain ground when jumping smoothly and meeting his fences right, and these gains can amount to many lengths at the end of a three-mile race.

After a few schools over hurdles the horse should be ridden at a good half speed over small 'chase fences. Schooling fences should be much smaller than those on any racecourse, but they must be stiff, with good guard rails at the bottom, and there should be at least one with an open ditch. It is a mistake to school over big fences; even horses being schooled for the National never jump big fences during schooling. Boots or bandages should be worn to protect legs from blows and possible over-reaches.

Indeed, careful attention must be paid to the legs, particularly in this early stage of jumping fast; and at the first sign of any heat or swelling, fast work should be stopped and remedial measures taken. This fast work should be kept at half pace, and it will be some time before we ask the horse fully to extend himself, certainly not until he is really fit and galloping well on the flat.

Races are won in the stable, which means good feeding, good grooming, good exercise. Every horse must be treated as an individual, but most hunters should be taken off hunting at least six weeks before their first race. Some horses run up very light and need longer, but if your horse is in good hard condition and reasonably well covered a period of two weeks to build him up and prepare him for the strenuous work ahead should be sufficient. During this time most of his work, about two hours a day, should be slow; walk and slow trot on the roads is what is wanted, and the more gentle hills that can be included the better. Feeding depends again on the individual, but the most important rule is to feed the best: the best hay and the best oats. 14 lb. of good hay a day and about 10 lb. of corn, mixed with bran and chaff, damped down, and fed in four feeds a day, plus plenty of fresh water, which must always be available, is the sort of diet needed.

After two weeks, faster work should begin: long canters and schooling over hurdles at half pace, keeping the horse well within himself. The hay ration should now be gradually reduced and the oats increased in proportion. For a reduction of 4 lb. of hay increase the corn ration by 2 lb.

At the end of the second two weeks he should be doing a half-speed gallop, up to six furlongs, three times a week, with a school over fences at the same pace. It is most important at this stage that the horse is not allowed to go 'all out'. It is bad for the legs, and is likely to put a horse off his feed. Give long transitions from canter into half-speed gallop, holding the pace for six furlongs, then take time in reducing the pace back to a long rein walk. Then dismount, slacken girths and walk home. This work is best done in company with at least one other horse.

In the last two weeks we must sharpen the horse, to clear his wind and teach him how to sprint. He should be galloped at half speed for $1\frac{1}{2}$ miles and extended for the last two furlongs, and he will also need a sharp school over fences. Three gallops should be ridden during the first of these two weeks, every other day, with quiet work in between. The difficulty in getting a horse fit is in giving him the necessary work without getting him bored or excited, depending on his temperament.

A horse will show in the stable how his work is affecting him. If he is eating up and is contented and happy three sharp schools a week during this period will suit him. If he is off his feed and restless, he should be led out on his easy days and allowed to pick at grass, but if he eats up at night there is not much wrong, although the nervous or highly strung horse may need only two sharp schools a week. A horse should sweat healthily during his gallops and his breathing should be deep and even. At the end of a gallop warm clothing should be waiting, and it should be put on immediately – a chill is the easiest thing to catch.

Throughout this period the going must be watched with great care. In February and March it can be hard from frost or deep from rain, both of which make the ground unsuitable for fast work. Good, even going with plenty of old thick grass to give a resilient cover should be sought for diligently if work is not to be interrupted.

The jockey will not do a horse justice unless he or she is racing fit, which is very different from being hunting fit. Having to ride with a much shorter stirrup and to sit up against a galloping horse for over three miles puts strain on muscles you rarely use. Riding work twice a week with any racehorse trainer who will co-operate is one of the best ways of toning up these muscles.

As in show jumping, your horse's first performance in public should be a happy one, and therefore his first race should be made easy. It takes a horse many days to recover from a hard-ridden race, so he will be less liable to suffer from nerves in the future if his introduction is a gentle one. The best advice one can give to a beginner is to get away to a good start, well up with the field, then allow the horse to settle down to the pace he knows and likes, and stay in it, regardless of the rest of the field. This, in my experience, is the way to ride the first race on any novice. Before riding a race, always walk the course so that you may note any rough or heavy going, any gradients, where your horse must be allowed to take his time, or bends that are unusually sharp. Try to visualise a track that will let you ride the shortest distance possible, and always try to give your horse a clear run into his fence. If a fence is hit hard it takes a great deal out of the horse; it upsets the rhythm of his stride and, even more important, the rhythm of his breathing; so if he should hit a fence, let him go really steady until he has recovered. Until you are experienced do not attempt to use your whip – more races have been lost by the inexpert use of the whip on the run in than have ever been won. Ride your race on the principle of minimum movement; the more still you can sit, in balance with your horse, the less you will take out of him, and if you are riding a finish do it with your legs and hands. Finally, most amateur trainers over-gallop their horses in training. Avoid fast work until the horse is ready, otherwise something will go bad on you and your horse may well be laid up for half the season.

Chapter 8

TRAINING FOR ONE- AND THREE-DAY EVENTS

To quote a British Horse Society pamphlet: 'The objects of Combined Training are to show the rider's spirit, boldness and knowledge of training and conditioning his horse, to obtain the best performance across country, and to show the handiness, courage, jumping ability, stamina and speed of the well trained horse.' These are admirable aims, and there is no doubt that in the twenty years or so of 'eventing' in this country the standard of general horsemanship has improved beyond belief. There are three main types of combined training. The Three-Day Event, comprising dressage, speed, endurance, cross-country and show jumping, on three successive days; One-Day Horse Trials, which comprise dressage, jumping and cross-country, and Combined Competitions, which consist of a dressage test and a show-jumping competition.

ONE-DAY EVENTS – Undoubtedly the one-day horse trial is the most popular. In the current year about forty of these events are being held throughout the country. There are three grades, depending on how much money the horse has won: Novice, Intermediate and Advanced classes. I want to deal, in some detail, with preparing a horse for the novice competition.

86

Any horse that has been schooled successfully on the lines
that I have laid down in these chapters should be able to
negotiate the three phases of a novice horse trial. The dressage
test is simplicity itself and is designed to show that the horse
is being schooled on the right lines. First, the horse must be
calm; second, he must be in front of the legs and on the bit;
third, his basic paces must be correct; and lastly he must
show energy, submission and suppleness. Now, the horse has
been trained for the last twelve months or more with these
aims in view, but he will obviously need some brushing up
in his schooling on the flat and over show fences if we have
been hunting him regularly. Therefore much the same procedure as for the point-to-point horse must be followed. Let
us say that we are aiming for a One-Day Event in April; then
we must stop hunting in early February at the latest and let
the horse down slowly in feed for a few days, riding only slow
exercise to give him a chance to recuperate from his hunting
and to build him up into robust condition. Although the
dressage test for novice horse trials is a very simple one, the
trainer's approach to it must be methodical and patient. I say
patient because during the hunting season one is inclined to
allow accurate schooling to slide. So the horse has got to
be re-introduced to a confined space of 40 metres by 20
metres quietly and with care. A marked manège, bounded by
4 in. high white boarding is a necessary facility if you are
going to treat horse trials seriously. Many well-bred horses
take part in horse trials today, and many of them go clear in
the cross-country phase but let themselves down badly in the
dressage and the show jumping. This is usually due to bad
initial training and insufficient preparation before the actual
day. There are 110 good marks to be gained in the dressage
test, and your horse and rider should be given every chance
to secure as many of these as possible. Use your manège only

when your horse is well settled – after the morning road work, for instance. Horses vary considerably, but it is a golden rule never to introduce something new to a fresh horse. Always enter your manège correctly and leave it in the same manner 'A', and not by walking over the boards as I have often seen thoughtless people do.

To begin with, walk down the centre line on a long rein and halt at 'X' each time you enter. Stand still for a few seconds, give your horse a pat, and then walk straight forward. For the first few days all work in the manège should be done at the walk on a long rein, until your horse will perform circles, half-circles, inclines and halts calmly and quietly. Very soon your horse will learn that he is confined by the white boards, and he should eventually walk round the manège on a loose rein without any indication from the rider. Having achieved calmness, we can begin to ask a little more. All the exercises that were done at the walk, except for half-circles, can now be carried out at ordinary trot. Aim at an active pace with even rhythm. Maintain this rhythm on changes of direction, and on circles, whether rising or sitting. Make certain your horse bends correctly on circles and when riding through the corners. This will gradually improve his suppleness to right and left. Transitions – halt, walk, trot; trot, walk, halt – all done with a light contact and steady head carriage, will promote smoothness in change of pace and help to bring him onto the bit and in front of the legs. Lengthening and shortening the stride in trot will improve his cadence and flexibility. Aim for more accuracy in each movement; leave the side of the school as your body passes the marker on circles and inclines, and don't overshoot when turning down the centre line. All this calls for the correct positioning of your horse well before the movement. Do not be in a hurry to canter, or your horse may become unbalanced, fall round the corners and even become disunited. Wait until he is doing all your suppling exercises at ordinary trot smoothly and fluently, plus cavalletti work, before attempting to canter in the manège. Return then to the basic schooling over cavalletti. This will make your horse think, and it will improve his accuracy, suppleness and balance. During your short periods in the manège work your horse back to the standard of leg yielding on the circle and a little shoulder-in in trot down the long side. This will improve his hock action and straightness.

In the manège your object is to obtain calmness with energy and accuracy: true basic paces, in fact. Do not neglect your own position and the application of the aids. It is a good idea to get an experienced person to criticise your riding as frequently as you can, because it is very difficult to check and correct your own faults.

On the day of the competition your horse must be worked in for his test. This means he must be exercised, settled down or warmed up, according to his temperament. Whatever work he requires, it is too late at this eleventh hour to 'teach' him anything. If an attempt is made to improve a movement at this point all one succeeds in doing is upsetting and confusing the horse, and in getting the rider into a state of nerves into the bargain. Therefore, ride in according to his requirements and then walk about on a long rein for the last few minutes before entering the arena.

You should know the test and all the rules relating to it, so well that you do not have to think about it. When you ride down the centre line, look forward, make your transition to halt early rather than late and *smile* when you salute!

Although we do a great deal of work both on the flat and over small fences in trot, remember the horse must now be schooled to gallop over his fences. In the show jumping phase the novice speed is 300 metres (327 yards) a minute. This is not very fast, but it still means that the novice must learn to jump boldly and make tight turns in good balance. A judgement of pace and speed needs to be developed, and this is best done by galloping a measured distance against a stop watch. It is quite wrong to use up a great deal of energy by going too fast in the show jumping when there is a strenuous cross-country to follow; so learn to judge your horse's speed and pace so that he will gallop and jump economically. When his cavalletti work has reached the stage of being calm but active, start work over grids and combinations to increase his precision and to improve his style. Start your grid with two rails 2 ft. high and about 10 ft. apart, depending on the stride of your horse. Approach at a balanced trot, and canter the last one or two strides. Gradually increase the number of rails until your horse is jumping six rails 10 ft. apart in good balance. The rider should sit passively, weight nicely forward as in all cavalletti work. When used properly, this grid will quicken the take-off and improve the elasticity. The distance between rails can be altered according to whether your horse flattens his back or gets too close to his fences and climbs over. Good use can be made of a double to make him bascule over his fences, using parallel rails 2 ft. high and 2 ft. apart with another true parallel 3 ft. by 3 ft. placed 24 ft. away from the first. This is the easiest form of double with one reasonable stride. As your horse becomes confident increase the spread to 4 ft. and the inside distance between fences to 25 ft. 6 in. In the novice class show jumping the fences cannot exceed 3 ft. 9 in., which is no great height to jump. What the trainer must concentrate on is the horse going well between fences, so lay out a course with simple turns and changes of direction, as we did in our early schooling. Keep fences low and don't jump too many of them. Little and often at this stage is a good motto.

The novice cross-country course should be well within the ability of a well-trained hunter, if our preparation after we have stopped hunting is on sound lines. No fence is higher than 3 ft. 6 in. but the speed of 575 yds. a minute is quite a fast galloping pace in which to jump 16 to 20 fences, and it means that most of your fences must be jumped at a faster pace than normal. First of all, get an idea of this by clocking your horse over a measured distance. If this speed is too fast for your horse to jump safely and happily across country in his present state of training, then it would be foolhardy to attempt it and risk spoiling a good horse. Too many people make the mistake of pushing their horse too hard in early one-day events, and always with disastrous results. As in our first show jumping competition, this must be a happy association, so ride across country keeping your horse well within himself. A good galloping stride must be aimed at, with your horse standing well back from his fences, but not a pace that will unbalance and exhaust him. The rider should try to sit as still as possible and to guide, control and balance, allowing the horse to jump from his stride, with the minimum of interference. Walk the course and study each fence; the approach, the landing and the getaway.

Riding uphill or downhill, the rider must keep his weight forward so that there is complete freedom for the loins; and his hands must be light with a stretched rein, allowing full play of the head and neck. Incidentally, a neckstrap for uphill work is indispensable. When jumping downhill, provided that the horse is kept straight, the hocks will be well under the body by virtue of the slope, and the horse will be inclined to stand off. When jumping uphill, any tendency to rush the hill should be checked, and the pace, canter or trot should be slow and controlled. The horse will tend to come in close to his fence, but with fences at this height no harm will be done. Jumping into water is unnatural to most horses and is an act of obedience. By commonsense training, using a small pond, it can be taught quite quickly. As soon as a horse realises there is a firm base for his feet below the water his fear disappears. Make certain, therefore, that your stream has a firm base by walking in it yourself before asking your horse to do so. It is also a wise precaution to rake the bottom to remove sharp stones. Teach your horse first to walk through, either by leading him or by taking him in company with an older horse. First teach him to walk, then to trot through. When he is quite bold at this and will enter the water without hesitation, put a low rail on the far bank jumping *out* of the water. Eventually, a rail can be placed on the near bank so that he enters the water by a jump. Some trainers like to put a small fence in the middle of the stream, but I have not found this necessary.

In competition the rider must be careful to reduce his speed, especially when the water is deep, because, on landing in the water the sudden check to the horse's pace is liable to turn him over, which is something that can often happen with an impetuous horse. Your schooling fences for cross-country work need to be solid and formidable looking; they need not be big, but they should be well-sited and they should include as many different types as you have money and space to build. Most schooling fences should fit in with their natural surroundings when possible, but the trainer should also school his horse over unusual fences purely as an obedience test. Narrow frontage post-and-rails with a strand of string at either side to represent wire is an example, steps up and down and the coffin type of fence are all good for obedience tests. Taking part in one-day horse trials calls for a good standard of riding and training, but novice horse trials are well within the scope of the average performer, and if a methodical system of schooling is adhered to a great deal of pleasure and satisfaction can be enjoyed with a horse of no more than medium ability.

THREE-DAY EVENTS – There is a very large gap between the one-day trial horse and the three-day event horse, but it is not so much in the training as in the basic requirements of the animal. The three-day event is a test of courage and stamina, speed and training. In the higher competitions it is the thoroughbred that can produce these qualities. But it must be a horse with the temperament to accept this training. As we have said earlier, no longer can one get away with a bad dressage test and make it up on the second day. The type of horse likely to do well in three-day events must first of all have quality and he must be a thoroughbred or a near-thoroughbred, preferably from a hunter-'chaser line. This will mean he can stay, that he is fast and should have the second essential, which is a good temperament – an absolutely vital quality if he is going to accept willingly the schooling on the flat and over show fences. The third essential is fitness. How much work can a horse take? Just as important is the ability of the trainer, who must be experienced enough to work his horses up to a peak of fitness. The fitness of a race-horse is the absolute maximum in preparation, the horse being strung up to exert himself to the maximum possible extent over a comparatively short distance. But this is not quite what is wanted in the event horse, even though a great deal can be learnt from the conditioning of a racehorse that will be applicable to the eventer.

THE DRESSAGE TEST – The FEI Three-Day Event Test, which is done in the full-sized arena 60 metres by 20 metres, is designed to show the stages that the horse has passed through in his training up to this standard. All the movements, with the exception of the half-pass, have been done in our training programme. If the shoulder-in at trot is good, the half-pass at trot will follow fairly easily. The mistake most trainers make in teaching the half-pass is that they consider their horse must go sideways, and this they aim to make him to do by crossing his legs. In the true half-pass the horse goes obliquely forward by putting one leg across the front of the other, which is quite different from crossing his legs. The body is straight, the forehand leads slightly and the horse is flexed towards the direction of movement. The flexion is so small that it is better in the early stages to keep the horse straight, so that there is less likelihood of losing impulsion and getting an irregular movement. The best time to practise the half-pass is on the way home after morning exercise. Two or three steps across a country lane soon teaches the elements of this movement, and it can then be perfected in the manège.

In this test the horse is expected to show accuracy and impulsion, to go freely forward and to accept his bridle happily. Transitions may be progressive but they must be smooth, with no resistance from the mouth. Each corner of the manège is a quarter circle, and he must ride through his corners correctly bent and with impulsion. He must halt well, remaining in front of the legs and up to the bit. If he cannot halt well, in a balanced manner, he will certainly fail in his rein back. He must be calm – he must be straight. It goes without saying that the rider must know the test so thoroughly that he can see two movements ahead, so that he may plan, to position his horse for each. The best way to learn a long test is by sketching it on a piece of paper at odd times during the day, and then walking the test on your own feet in the manège.

In preparing your horse for the test, anticipation is one of the great dangers, and it is best to practise movements and transitions in small groups and not in the order of the test. The second danger is boredom. To flog away in a manège until the horse becomes bored and loses all brilliance and joy from his movements is to defeat the objects of schooling. The closer you are to a competition, the less time should be spent in the manège. If the basic schooling has been carefully and methodically carried out, this test should hold no terrors for the average good horse and rider.

THE SECOND DAY – Phases A and C are Roads and Tracks, which must be carried out at a speed of 262 yards a minute. This speed is too fast for ordinary trot and too slow for ordinary canter. To extend the trot takes too much out of the horse. Teach your horse to canter quietly on a long rein, then study the roads and tracks phases and decide where the going is good enough to canter. Many marks have been lost by treating this phase lightheartedly.

Jumping at speed has already been discussed. In the steeple chase phase our speed is 656 yards a minute, and to gain maximum bonus we must ride the two-mile steeplechase course at about 25 miles an hour. Judgement of speed and pace is essential, so careful work must be done beforehand with the stopwatch. To arrive eventually at this speed and still keep your horse calm, long transitions must be practised. Starting with a basic speed of 400 yards a minute for a quarter of a mile, gradually increase until 700 yards a minute is achieved. In the final stages of training, short bursts of 800 yards a minute can be attempted. Decreasing speed again should always be done through a long transition.

The speed in the cross-country phase is not as fast as for a one-day event but the course is much longer and the fences are usually more formidable. An average speed of about 20 miles an hour is necessary if you are to gain maximum bonus. Your horse's cross-country ability will be improved by experience in one-day horse trials, gradually increasing the difficulty of the events you enter him for, and by careful schooling over specialised fences at home. Emphasis should be placed on increasing the impressiveness or trickiness of a particular obstacle gradually. If he is very fit, a horse that jumps boldly and one that is taught to be versatile will find no difficulty in the actual obstacles. Maintaining the speed is a greater difficulty, because there are many fences that must be jumped slowly, such as a drop, or disaster will follow. A careful study of the ground and of each fence, to decide where time can be made up, is of the utmost importance.

However good your horsemastership at the end of the second day, however much massaging, rubbing down and bandaging you have done, your horse is bound to be tired and stiff on the morning of the third day. The object of the show jumping test on the third day is to prove that 'on the day after a severe test of endurance, horses have retained the suppleness, energy and obedience necessary for them to continue in service'.

A quiet walk out for twenty minutes, to stretch muscles and test for soundness on the morning of the third day starts the preparation for the final test. Before the competition, work up gradually to lateral suppling exercises, ride large circles at walk and trot; lengthen and shorten the stride at trot; practice smaller circles and lengthen and shorten stride at the canter. Finish up by jumping the practice fence without attempting to adjust the stride. On the previous day your horse has been jumping fast and boldly, therefore he has been jumping big. Any attempt to change this radically is courting disaster. Each fence must be jumped according to its merit, but no fence is over 4 ft. high and many are much smaller, therefore your pace must be slower than on the previous day. But if you keep your horse balanced you can let him jump big without any particular attention being attached to placing. Choose and ride a track, however, that will make your turns and changes of direction as easy as possible.

Chapter 9

CONCLUSION

In schooling a young horse, the trainer's aim for the first
year should be to make his pupil as versatile as possible. His
education must be broadly based, and whatever the ultimate
goal, whether it be hunter, racehorse, show jumper, polo
pony or just a riding horse, his training must proceed along
the lines and proven principles of advanced equitation. If any
trainer attempts to specialise too soon and misses out certain
logical steps in this sequence of training, progress will cease.
The horse will become confused, he will start to put up
evasions and resistances that become more and more difficult
to eradicate until, eventually, the inexperienced trainer
resorts to force, and that will be the end of any further
progress.

So proceed methodically with the basic principles that I
have outlined here. It is impossible to lay down a fixed time-
table because so much depends on the ability and experience
of the trainer and on the fitness and temperament of the
young horse. Most trainers, unfortunately, try to go too fast,
not appreciating that the best policy is to proceed steadily,
never attempting a new lesson until the previous one is well
understood. As a general rule I would say the first year
should be considered as the time required to produce a young
horse with a natural carriage; strong enough to balance him-

self and the weight of his rider across easy country and on simple school movements and to jump a variety of small fences, both natural and coloured, from trot and canter without fuss or excitement. He should go freely forward from the leg and carry himself without leaning on the reins, should move away from other horses without hesitation and approach them without fuss. He should stand still to be mounted and dismounted, and he should be quiet and easy to handle in the stable and outside.

The trainer must be methodical in his daily work; always making a new lesson easy for the horse by first repeating all the things he has already learnt. This will make him receptive and confident. Then you can start your new lesson, and if you progress a little, be satisfied.

In the second year you can work from sound beginnings. Your horse will begin to show a natural aptitude, and from this you can decide what his particular line will be.

Finally, a word about condition and exercise. It is the trainer's task not only to school his young horse but also to improve and develop its bodily health and fitness. The correct amount of good quality food combined with sufficient healthy exercise, continued over a long period, is the only answer. The young horse when he first comes for training may be fat and well rounded and full of himself. This may confuse the inexperienced. Condition of this kind is not fitness. The flesh is flabby and fat, and to transform this into hard tough muscle is a gradual process that cannot be hurried. The young horse in this state is unable to stand severe exertion. If he is overworked the muscles of a horse in this fat condition soon loses elasticity, throwing extra weight onto the tendons and joints with a resultant straining and bruising. Working tired horses when unfit is the beginning of all their leg troubles. To build up good hard muscle the work and training must at first be light but spread over a longish period of the day. The longer your young horse is in the fresh air each day the better for his general health, his respiration and his digestion. Two short schooling periods a day are, in fact better than one, and two hours in a paddock where he will quietly exercise himself are essential. The bulk of his exercise should be done at the walk, and he will get a large amount of walking exercise if he is allowed a couple of hours a day in a paddock. A moderate amount of schooling should be done at the trot and eventually a little in canter will begin to harden the flabby muscles. Any attempt to cut short this early hardening process will result in loss of flesh and a loss of general condition.

So the trainer must look at his horses not only outside the stable, but inside as well. The quantities of feed required cannot be put into a book. This can only be learned by observation and experience, but by sticking to a good routine of feeding and exercise a healthy, happy and well-trained mount will be the ultimate result, and he will give you many years of pleasure.

INDEX

accuracy, on approach to fences, 37, 51, 76

back,
    examination of, 4
    muscles, 32
    relaxation of, in jumping, 38, 48
    suppleness of, 42, 45
balance,
    adjustment to rider, 24
    cantering, 33, 34, 35, 36
    jumping, 18, 25, 36, 47–9, 52, 66, 68–9, 71, 97
    on the lunge, 8, 9, 25
    pace changes, 31
    rider, 21–3, 37
    trotting, 8–10, 12, 28, 32
    turning, 34–9
    undulating country, 30–1
    walking over trotting poles, 27
bandages, 82, 96
bascule, 12, 36, 90
bevelling, 4
bit, 24, 29, 42–3, 45, 46, 73, 94
boots, 82
bran, 83
bruising, 99
buying, 3–4

canter aid, 34, 35, 54–5
cantering,
    action of horse, 33–4, 54
    avoidance of early, 20, 33
    balanced, 54
    cavalletti, 35–7

in circles, 37–9, 42
in early mounted training, 35–7, 42–4
loose jumping, 16, 17, 25
on landing, 58–9
on the lunge, 11–12, 25
over undulating country, 43, 51
cavalletti, 10, 34–6, 48–9, 57–8, 62, 74, 90
cavesson, 5, 7, 10
chaff, 83
chambron, 45
cheekpiece, 4, 33
chills, 84
circles,
    cantering in, 35, 38–9, 42–3
    changing legs in, 43–4
    flying change in, 60–1
    in early mounted training, 29–30, 32
    jumping on, 10, 58–9
    shoulder in, 40–2, 59
    transitions in, 53–5
    walking in, 6, 7–8
clock, riding against, 72–3
conformation, 3, 45
corn, 5, 83
corns, 73
counter-canter, 44, 55–6
course construction, 65–8, 90–1
courses, jumping small, 51–6
crib-biting, 21
cross-country riding, 51, 87, 90, 91–2
    see also hunting; roads and tracks

INDEX

diagonal aid, 61

diet *see* feeding

direction, change of, 7, 27, 39, 58–60, 69–70, 72, 90, 97

dismounting, 25, 99

distance, measuring of, 47–8, 57, 62–4, 67

double bridle, 79

draw reins, 45

dressage, 23, 24, 60, 75, 87–9, 93–5

ears, 2

exercise, 25, 53–4, 73, 83–4, 99–100

see also jumping, exercises

eyes, 2, 4

feeding, 4, 5, 7, 19, 73, 83, 84, 87, 99, 100

feet, examination of, 4–5

fences,
  approach to, 36–8, 59, 68, 82
  combinations, 67–8, 90
  cross-country, 90–2
  distance, 15, 38, 67, 68, 90
  distance from trotting poles, 36
  doubles, 17, 48
  grids, use of, 90
  height, 12, 17, 36, 50–1, 62, 65–6, 90, 91
  introduction to, 7, 12
  jumping at speed, 81–2
  making and siting, 74, 79, 81–2, 92
  manège, 15–16, 17–18
  parallel, 17, 37–8, 57, 62, 65–8
  solidity of, 16, 62, 74
  spread, 12, 14, 17, 50, 62, 66, 90
  staircase, 65, 66
  table, 79
  vertical, 65, 66–7
  water, 65, 66–7
  width, 50, 62
  see also course construction

fidgeting, 26

figure eight, 39–40, 43, 58–9

fitness, 32, 73, 81, 83, 84–5, 93, 96, 99

flying change, 55, 58–61, 70

forelegs, protection of, 7

forward movement *see* leading

gallop, 77, 78, 83–4, 90, 91

girth, 34, 41, 48

grooming, 83

half-pass, 94

haltering, 4

halting, 5, 7–8, 12, 16, 31, 94

hands, 5, 23–4, 34, 39, 41, 46, 47–8

hay, 83

head,
  position in jumping, 47–8, 82
  related to balance, 31, 45

head carriage, 18, 28–9, 30–3, 38, 42–3, 45–6, 79, 88

hearing, 4
  see also voice

hindquarters, 31, 32–3, 38, 42

hip, 16, 46

hock action, 9, 31, 32, 89

hocks, 12, 27, 28, 31, 36, 38, 46, 79, 91

hounds, familiarity with, 76–7

hunting, 3, 18, 76–9, 83, 97

impulsion,
  change of direction, 27
  in shoulder-in, 41
  in trotting, 28
  in work on circle, 39–40
  rider's control, 47, 52
  stride variation, 67, 68, 69

inclines, 32

jaw, 45, 79

joints, 78, 99

jumping,
  at an angle, 57, 72
  downhill, 91

early mounted, 20, 35
exercises, 53, 57–60
from a trot, 25, 28, 35–8, 47,
    51, 52, 58, 62, 77
from a walk, 27
horse's action in, 47–8
improvements in, 47–9
loose, 14, 16–18, 72
on the circle, 58–9
on the lunge, 7, 10–13, 14, 25
rider's action in, 48–9
speed in, 48, 81–2, 91–2, 94–5
straight, 82
stride length in, 15, 38, 47,
    48–9
uphill, 91–2
jump-off, 73

kicking, 19

landing, getaway on, 66, 91
lateral movement, 32–3, 40–2
leading, 1, 5–6
legs,
    care of horse's, 4–5, 82–3
    rider's, 21–3, 24, 30, 33, 34,
    37–9, 41
lessons, length of, 5, 8, 10, 17, 32,
    100
loin muscles, 29–30, 32, 45, 56
loins, 22, 29, 39, 42, 46, 91
loose jumping see jumping, loose
lungeing, 3, 7–10, 19, 25
lungeing whip, 6, 16–17

manège, 14–17, 25, 40, 87–8, 89,
    94
mounted training, 3, 19–21
    see also schooling on the flat
mounting, 25, 99
mouth, 4, 23–4, 28–9, 31, 33, 37,
    39, 78, 94
muscle development, 7, 18, 24,
    25, 27, 28–9, 32, 78, 99–100

neck,
    position in cantering, 33

position in jumping, 47–8, 82
position on trotting, 29
related to balance, 18, 27, 31,
    45
neck muscles, 29–30, 32, 45, 56
noseband, 4
nuts, 16

oats, 16, 17, 83
obedience,
    importance of, 2, 4
    in early lessons, 5, 6, 7, 8, 10
    in early mounted training, 20,
    24, 25, 31, 32, 53
    in galloping, 78
    in hunting, 76, 77
    in show jumping, 72, 74
    in strike-off, 38
    re-establishment of, 74
one-day events, 87–93

pace,
    change of, 72, 88
    decrease in, 31, 45, 52
    in early mounted training, 16,
    38
    in lungeing, 7
    in rein back, 46
    in show jumping, 18
    judgement of, 67, 68, 90–1
    see also impulsion; transitions
point-to-points, 81–5
prancing, 26
punishment, 2, 21, 26, 55

racehorses, 72, 99
refusals, 13, 69, 71, 73, 74
rein back, 46, 94
rein changing, 16
rewards, 12, 16, 51
rib cage, 22, 38
roads and tracks, 94–6
rushing, 27, 47, 62, 92

saddle, 73
schooling on the flat, 24–6, 51

schooling whip, 5–6, 27
scope, 7, 18, 21–3, 36, 38–9, 47–8, 52, 61, 78–9
seat, rider's, 21–3, 36, 38–9, 47–8, 52, 61, 78–9
serpentines, 32, 55
shoes, shoeing, 4, 73
shoulder, 16, 42, 89
shoulder-in, 40–2
show jumping, 3, 65–75, 87, 89–93, 96–7
shying, 13, 26
side reins, 46
snaffle, 6–7, 46, 79
soreness, 4, 13, 73
speed,
　in competitions, 72, 90–1, 95–6
　length of stride, 67
　on entering water, 92
　take-off, 51
　see also pace; sprinting
spine, 29, 46
spiral, 40, 70
spoiling, 4, 20
stable vices, 19
staleness, 73
stamina, 26, 87
standing, 4, 7–8, 25
steeplechases, 81, 86
stiffness, 73, 96
stifle, 46
stirrups, 22–3, 36, 37, 82, 84
strain, 4–5
stride adjustment, 18, 27, 31, 38, 42, 47–9, 52, 55, 57, 66–70
stride control, 18
strides,
　between fences, 15, 38, 47–9
　seeing, 49, 61–4
strike-off, 34, 35, 38, 61
sugar, 17
suppleness,
　counter-canter, 44

exercise in circles, 10, 32, 34, 38–43
lateral, 27, 29–30, 96
longitudinal, 27, 29–30, 45
rein back, 46

take-off, take-off zone, 4, 49, 50–1, 57, 62, 66, 72, 81
teeth, 4
tendons, 4, 78, 99
three-day events, 25, 86, 93–9
throatlatch, 5
trainer, qualities needed, 1–2, 20–1
training programme, 19
transitions, 11, 31, 34, 43–4, 53–5, 78, 88, 96, 99
trotting,
　action of horse in, 28–9
　balance, 8–10, 12, 28
　balanced, 10, 34, 39, 40–1, 58, 90
　change of legs in, 43–4
　extended, 32, 40
　in early mounted training, 16, 20, 25, 28–32
　over poles, 8–10, 12, 14, 17, 29, 35–8
　rising, 28, 30, 35
　sitting, 28, 30, 38
　see also jumping, from a trot
trotting poles, 8–10, 12, 14, 16, 27, 29, 36–7, 47

voice, used in training, 1, 4–6, 16, 25–6

walking, 6, 7–8, 10, 12, 16–17, 20, 26–7, 31, 35
water, entering, 92
　see also fences, water
weaving, 19
wind-sucking, 19
withers, 22, 29, 75

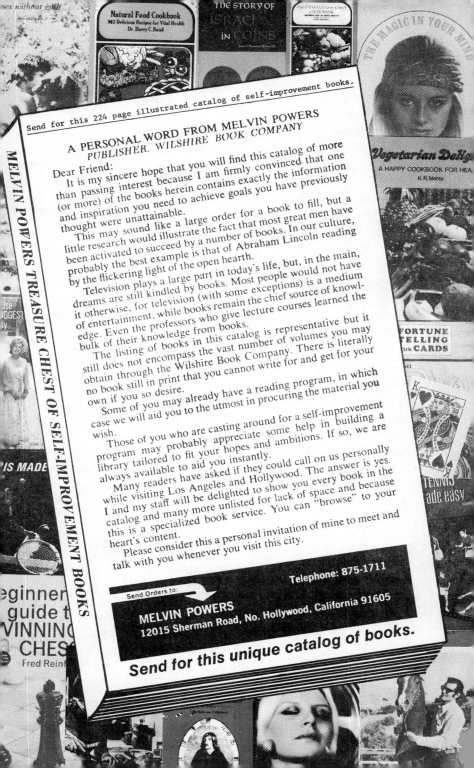

Melvin Powers
SELF-IMPROVEMENT
LIBRARY

<table>
<tr><td>ABILITY TO LOVE Dr. Allan Fromme</td><td>$2.00</td></tr>
<tr><td>ACT YOUR WAY TO SUCCESSFUL LIVING Neil & Margaret Rau</td><td>2.00</td></tr>
<tr><td>ADVANCED TECHNIQUES OF HYPNOSIS Melvin Powers</td><td>1.00</td></tr>
<tr><td>ANIMAL HYPNOSIS Dr. F. A. Völgyesi</td><td>2.00</td></tr>
<tr><td>ASTROLOGY: A FASCINATING HISTORY P. Naylor</td><td>2.00</td></tr>
<tr><td>ASTROLOGY: HOW TO CHART YOUR HOROSCOPE Max Heindel</td><td>2.00</td></tr>
<tr><td>ASTROLOGY: YOUR PERSONAL SUN-SIGN GUIDE Beatrice Ryder</td><td>2.00</td></tr>
<tr><td>ASTROLOGY FOR EVERYDAY LIVING Janet Harris</td><td>2.00</td></tr>
<tr><td>ASTROLOGY GUIDE TO GOOD HEALTH Alexandra Kayhle</td><td>2.00</td></tr>
<tr><td>ASTROLOGY MADE EASY Astarte</td><td>2.00</td></tr>
<tr><td>ASTROLOGY MADE PRACTICAL Alexandra Kayhle</td><td>2.00</td></tr>
<tr><td>ASTROLOGY, ROMANCE, YOU AND THE STARS Anthony Novell</td><td>2.00</td></tr>
<tr><td>BEGINNER'S GUIDE TO WINNING CHESS Fred Reinfeld</td><td>2.00</td></tr>
<tr><td>BICYCLING FOR FUN AND GOOD HEALTH Kenneth E. Luther</td><td>2.00</td></tr>
<tr><td>BOOK OF TALISMANS, AMULETS & ZODIACAL GEMS William Pavitt</td><td>3.00</td></tr>
<tr><td>BRIDGE BIDDING MADE EASY Edwin Kantar</td><td>5.00</td></tr>
<tr><td>BRIDGE CONVENTIONS Edwin Kantar</td><td>4.00</td></tr>
<tr><td>CHECKERS MADE EASY Tom Wiswell</td><td>2.00</td></tr>
<tr><td>CHESS IN TEN EASY LESSONS Larry Evans</td><td>2.00</td></tr>
<tr><td>CHESS MADE EASY Milton L. Hanauer</td><td>1.00</td></tr>
<tr><td>CHESS MASTERY — A New Approach Fred Reinfeld</td><td>2.00</td></tr>
<tr><td>CHESS PROBLEMS FOR BEGINNERS edited by Fred Reinfeld</td><td>1.00</td></tr>
<tr><td>CHESS SECRETS REVEALED Fred Reinfeld</td><td>1.00</td></tr>
<tr><td>CHESS STRATEGY — An Expert's Guide Fred Reinfeld</td><td>2.00</td></tr>
<tr><td>CHESS TACTICS FOR BEGINNERS edited by Fred Reinfeld</td><td>1.00</td></tr>
<tr><td>CHESS THEORY & PRACTICE Morry & Mitchell</td><td>2.00</td></tr>
<tr><td>CHILDBIRTH WITH HYPNOSIS William S. Kroger, M.D.</td><td>2.00</td></tr>
<tr><td>COIN COLLECTING FOR BEGINNERS Burton Hobson & Fred Reinfeld</td><td>2.00</td></tr>
<tr><td>CONCENTRATION—A Guide to Mental Mastery Mouni Sadhu</td><td>2.00</td></tr>
<tr><td>CONVERSATION MADE EASY Elliot Russell</td><td>1.00</td></tr>
<tr><td>CULPEPER'S HERBAL REMEDIES Dr. Nicholas Culpeper</td><td>2.00</td></tr>
<tr><td>CYBERNETICS WITHIN US Y. Saparina</td><td>2.00</td></tr>
<tr><td>DOCTOR PSYCHO-CYBERNETICS Maxwell Maltz, M.D.</td><td>2.50</td></tr>
<tr><td>DOG TRAINING MADE EASY & FUN John W. Kellogg</td><td>2.00</td></tr>
<tr><td>DREAMS & OMENS REVEALED Fred Gettings</td><td>2.00</td></tr>
<tr><td>DR. LINDNER'S SPECIAL WEIGHT CONTROL METHOD</td><td>1.00</td></tr>
<tr><td>DYNAMIC THINKING Melvin Powers</td><td>1.00</td></tr>
<tr><td>ENCYCLOPEDIA OF MODERN SEX &
    LOVE TECHNIQUES R. Macandrew</td><td>2.00</td></tr>
<tr><td>EXAM SECRET Dennis B. Jackson</td><td>1.00</td></tr>
<tr><td>EXTRASENSORY PERCEPTION Simeon Edmunds</td><td>2.00</td></tr>
<tr><td>FAST GOURMET COOKBOOK Poppy Cannon</td><td>2.50</td></tr>
<tr><td>FORTUNE TELLING WITH CARDS P. Foli</td><td>2.00</td></tr>
<tr><td>GAYELORD HAUSER'S NEW GUIDE TO INTELLIGENT REDUCING</td><td>3.00</td></tr>
<tr><td>GOULD'S GOLD & SILVER GUIDE TO COINS Maurice Gould</td><td>2.00</td></tr>
<tr><td>GROW RICH WHILE YOU SLEEP Ben Sweetland</td><td>2.00</td></tr>
<tr><td>GUIDE TO DEVELOPING YOUR POTENTIAL Herbert A. Otto, Ph.D.</td><td>2.00</td></tr>
</table>

Melvin Powers
SELF-IMPROVEMENT
LIBRARY

_____GUIDE TO HAPPINESS *Dr. Maxwell S. Cagan* 2.00
_____GUIDE TO LIVING IN BALANCE *Frank S. Caprio, M.D.* 2.00
_____GUIDE TO RATIONAL LIVING *Albert Ellis, Ph.D. & R. Harper, Ph.D.* 2.00
_____GUIDE TO SUCCESSFUL MARRIAGE *Drs. Albert Ellis & R. Haper* 2.00
_____HANDWRITING ANALYSIS MADE EASY *John Marley* 2.00
_____HANDWRITING TELLS *Nadya Olyanova* 3.00
_____HARMONICA PLAYING FOR FUN & PROFIT *Hal Leighton* 2.00
_____HEALING POWER OF HERBS *May Bethel* 2.00
_____HELP YOURSELF TO BETTER SIGHT *Margaret Darst Corbett* 2.00
_____HELPING YOURSELF WITH APPLIED PSYCHOLOGY *R. Henderson* 2.00
_____HELPING YOURSELF WITH PSYCHIATRY *Frank S. Caprio, M.D.* 2.00
_____HERB HANDBOOK *Dawn MacLeod* 2.00
_____HERBS FOR COOKING AND HEALING *Dr. Donald Law* 2.00
_____HERBS FOR HEALTH How to Grow & Use Them *Louise Evans Doole* 2.00
_____HOME GARDEN COOKBOOK Delicious Natural Food Recipes *Ken Kraft* 3.00
_____HOW TO ATTRACT GOOD LUCK *A. H. Z. Carr* 2.00
_____HOW TO CONTROL YOUR DESTINY *Norvell* 2.00
_____HOW TO DEVELOP A BETTER SPEAKING VOICE *M. Hellier* 2.00
_____HOW TO DEVELOP A WINNING PERSONALITY *Martin Panzer* 2.00
_____HOW TO DEVELOP AN EXCEPTIONAL MEMORY *Young and Gibson* 2.00
_____HOW TO IMPROVE YOUR BRIDGE *Alfred Sheinwold* 2.00
_____HOW TO LIVE A RICHER & FULLER LIFE *Rabbi Edgar F. Magnin* 2.00
_____HOW TO MAKE MONEY IN REAL ESTATE *Stanley L. McMichael* 2.00
_____HOW TO OVERCOME YOUR FEARS *M. P. Leahy, M.D.* 2.00
_____HOW TO RAISE AN EMOTIONALLY HEALTHY,
         HAPPY CHILD *Albert Ellis, Ph.D.* 2.00
_____HOW TO SLEEP WITHOUT PILLS *Dr. David F. Tracy* 1.00
_____HOW TO SOLVE YOUR SEX PROBLEMS
         WITH SELF-HYPNOSIS *Frank S. Caprio, M.D.* 2.00
_____HOW TO STOP SMOKING THRU SELF-HYPNOSIS *Leslie M. LeCron* 2.00
_____HOW TO UNDERSTAND YOUR DREAMS *Geoffrey A. Dudley* 2.00
_____HOW TO USE AUTO-SUGGESTION EFFECTIVELY *John Duckworth* 2.00
_____HOW TO WIN AT CHECKERS *Fred Reinfeld* 2.00
_____HOW TO WIN AT POCKET BILLIARDS *Edward D. Knuchell* 2.00
_____HOW TO WIN AT POKER *Terence Reese & Anthony T. Watkins* 2.00
_____HOW YOU CAN BOWL BETTER USING SELF-HYPNOSIS *Jack Heise* 2.00
_____HOW YOU CAN HAVE CONFIDENCE AND POWER *Les Giblin* 2.00
_____HOW YOU CAN PLAY BETTER GOLF USING SELF-HYPNOSIS *Heise* 2.00
_____HOW YOU CAN STOP SMOKING PERMANENTLY *Ernest Caldwell* 1.00
_____HYPNOSIS AND SELF-HYPNOSIS *Bernard Hollander, M.D.* 2.00
_____HYPNOTISM *Carl Sextus* 2.00
_____HYPNOTISM & PSYCHIC PHENOMENA *Simeon Edmunds* 2.00
_____HYPNOTISM MADE EASY *Dr. Ralph Winn* 2.00
_____HYPNOTISM MADE PRACTICAL *Louis Orton* 2.00
_____HYPNOTISM REVEALED *Melvin Powers* 1.00
_____HYPNOTISM TODAY *Leslie LeCron & Jean Bordeaux, Ph.D.* 2.00
_____HYPNOTIST'S CASE BOOK *Alex Erskine* 1.00

Melvin Powers
SELF-IMPROVEMENT
LIBRARY

I WILL *Ben Sweetland*	2.00
ILLUSTRATED YOGA *William Zorn*	2.00
IMPOTENCE & FRIGIDITY *Edwin W. Hirsch, M.D.*	2.00
INCREASE YOUR LEARNING POWER *Geoffrey A. Dudley*	1.00
JUGGLING MADE EASY *Rudolf Dittrich*	1.00
LEFT-HANDED PEOPLE *Michael Barsley*	3.00
LSD — THE AGE OF MIND *Bernard Roseman*	2.00
MAGIC IN YOUR MIND *U. S. Andersen*	2.00
MAGIC MADE EASY *Byron Wels*	2.00
MAGIC OF NUMBERS *Robert Tocquet*	2.00
MAGIC OF THINKING BIG *Dr. David J. Schwartz*	2.00
MAGIC POWER OF YOUR MIND *Walter M. Germain*	2.00
MAGICIAN — His training and work *W. E. Butler*	2.00
MASTER KEYS TO SUCCESS, POPULARITY & PRESTIGE *C. W. Bailey*	2.00
MEDICAL HYPNOSIS HANDBOOK *Drs. Van Pelt, Ambrose, Newbold*	2.00
MEDITATION *Mouni Sadhu*	3.00
MENTAL POWER THRU SLEEP SUGGESTION *Melvin Powers*	1.00
MENTAL TELEPATHY EXPLAINED *Hereward Carrington*	.50
MIND OVER PLATTER *Peter G. Lindner, M.D.*	2.00
MODERN HYPNOSIS *Lesley Kuhn & Salvatore Russo, Ph.D.*	2.00
MODERN ISRAEL *Lily Edelman*	2.00
MODERN NUMEROLOGY *Morris C. Goodman*	2.00
MY WORLD OF ASTROLOGY *Sydney Omarr*	2.00
NATURAL FOOD COOKBOOK *Dr. Harry C. Bond*	2.00
NATURE'S MEDICINES *Richard Lucas*	2.00
NEW APPROACHES TO SEX IN MARRIAGE *John E. Eichelaub, M.D.*	2.00
NEW CARBOHYDRATE DIET COUNTER *Patti Lopez-Pereira*	1.00
NEW CONCEPTS OF HYPNOSIS *Bernard C. Gindes, M.D.*	3.00
NUMEROLOGY—ITS FACTS AND SECRETS *Ariel Yvon Taylor*	2.00
1001 BRILLIANT WAYS TO CHECKMATE *Fred Reinfeld*	2.00
1001 WINNING CHESS SACRIFICES & COMBINATIONS *Fred Reinfeld*	2.00
ORIENTAL SECRETS OF GRACEFUL LIVING *Boye De Mente*	1.00
OUR JEWISH HERITAGE *Rabbi Alfred Wolf & Joseph Gaer*	2.00
PALMISTRY MADE EASY *Fred Gettings*	2.00
PALMISTRY MADE PRACTICAL *Elizabeth Daniels Squire*	2.00
PALMISTRY SECRETS REVEALED *Henry Frith*	2.00
PEYOTE STORY *Bernard Roseman*	2.00
PIGEONS: HOW TO RAISE AND TRAIN THEM *William H. Allen, Jr.*	2.00
POST-HYPNOTIC INSTRUCTIONS *Arnold Furst*	2.00
How to give post-hypnotic suggestions for therapeutic purposes.	
PRACTICAL GUIDE TO BETTER CONCENTRATION *Melvin Powers*	2.00
PRACTICAL GUIDE TO PUBLIC SPEAKING *Maurice Forley*	2.00
PRACTICAL GUIDE TO SELF-HYPNOSIS *Melvin Powers*	2.00
PRACTICAL HYPNOTISM *Philip Magonet, M.D.*	1.00
PRACTICAL YOGA *Ernest Wood*	2.00
PROPHECY IN OUR TIME *Martin Ebon*	2.50
PSYCHEDELIC ECSTASY *William Marshall & Gilbert W. Taylor*	2.00

_____PSYCHO-CYBERNETICS *Maxwell Maltz, M.D.*   2.00
_____PSYCHOLOGY OF HANDWRITING *Nadya Olyanova*   2.00
_____PSYCHOSOMATIC GYNECOLOGY *William S. Kroger, M.D.*   10.00
_____ROMANCE OF HASSIDISM *Jacob S. Minkin*   2.50
_____SECRET OF BOWLING STRIKES *Dawson Taylor*   2.00
_____SECRET OF PERFECT PUTTING *Horton Smith & Dawson Taylor*   2.00
_____SECRET OF SECRETS *U. S. Andersen*   2.00
_____SECRETS OF HYPNOTISM *S. J. Van Pelt, M.D.*   2.00
_____SEEING INTO THE FUTURE *Harvey Day*   2.00
_____SELF-CONFIDENCE THROUGH SELF-ANALYSIS *E. Oakley*   1.00
_____SELF-HYPNOSIS Its Theory, Technique & Application *Melvin Powers*   2.00
_____SELF-HYPNOSIS A Conditioned-Response Technique *Laurance Sparks*   2.00
_____SERVICE OF THE HEART *Evelyn Garfield, Ph.D.*   2.50
_____7 DAYS TO FASTER READING *William S. Schaill*   2.00
_____SEW SIMPLY, SEW RIGHT *Mini Rhea & F. Leighton*   2.00
_____SEX & HUMAN BEHAVIOR BY NUMBERS *Alexandra Kayhle*   2.00
_____SEX AND HYPNOSIS *L. T. Woodward, M.D.*   2.00
_____SEX WITHOUT GUILT *Albert Ellis, Ph.D.*   2.00
_____SEXUALLY ADEQUATE FEMALE *Frank S. Caprio, M.D.*   2.00
_____SEXUALLY ADEQUATE MALE *Frank S. Caprio, M.D.*   2.00
_____STAMP COLLECTING FOR BEGINNERS *Burton Hobson*   2.00
_____STAMP COLLECTING FOR FUN & PROFIT *Frank Cetin*   1.00
_____STORY OF ISRAEL IN COINS *Jean & Maurice Gould*   2.00
_____STORY OF ISRAEL IN STAMPS *Maxim & Gabriel Shamir*   1.00
_____STUDENT'S GUIDE TO BETTER GRADES *J. A. Rickard*   2.00
_____STUDENT'S GUIDE TO EFFICIENT STUDY *D. E. James*   1.00
_____STUTTERING AND WHAT YOU CAN DO ABOUT IT *W. Johnson, Ph.D.*   2.00
_____SUCCESS-CYBERNETICS *U. S. Andersen*   2.00
_____TABLE TENNIS MADE EASY *Johnny Leach*   2.00
_____TAROT *Mouni Sadhu*   3.00
_____TAROT OF THE BOHEMIANS *Papus*   3.00
_____10 DAYS TO A GREAT NEW LIFE *William E. Edwards*   2.00
_____TENNIS MADE EASY *Joel Brecheen*   2.00
_____TEST YOUR ESP *Martin Ebon*   2.00
_____THERAPY THROUGH HYPNOSIS *edited by Raphael H. Rhodes*   2.00
_____THINK AND GROW RICH *Napoleon Hill*   2.00
_____THOUGHT DIAL *Sydney Omarr*   2.00
_____THREE MAGIC WORDS *U. S. Andersen*   2.00
_____TONGUE OF THE PROPHETS *Robert St. John*   3.00
_____TREASURY OF COMFORT *edited by Rabbi Sidney Greenberg*   2.00
_____TREASURY OF THE ART OF LIVING *edited by Rabbi S. Greenberg*   2.00
_____VEGETABLE GARDENING FOR BEGINNERS *Hugh Wiberg*   2.00
_____VEGETABLES FOR TODAY'S GARDENS *R. Milton Carleton*   2.00
_____VEGETARIAN COOKERY *Janet Walker*   2.00
_____VEGETARIAN COOKING MADE EASY & DELECTABLE *Veronica Vezza*   2.00
_____VEGETARIAN DELIGHTS — A Happy Cookbook for Health *K. R. Mehta*   2.00
_____VEGETARIAN GOURMET COOKBOOK *Joyce McKinnel*   2.00
_____WITCHCRAFT, MAGIC & OCCULTISM—A Fascinating History *W. B. Crow*   2.00
_____WITCHCRAFT—THE SIX SENSE *Justine Glass*   2.00
_____YOU ARE NOT THE TARGET *Laura Huxley*   2.00
_____YOU CAN ANALYZE HANDWRITING *Robert Holder*   2.00
_____YOU CAN LEARN TO RELAX *Dr. Samuel Gutwirth*   2.00
_____YOUR SUBCONSCIOUS POWER *Charles M. Simmons*   2.00
_____YOUR THOUGHTS CAN CHANGE YOUR LIFE *Donald Curtis*   2.00
_____YOUR WILL & WHAT TO DO ABOUT IT *Attorney Samuel G. Kling*   2.00
_____ZODIAC REVEALED *Rupert Gleadow*   2.00

Notes

Notes

Notes

Notes

Notes